S0-ARL-698

EV 4.00

Your Future Is
Your Friend

Merry Christmas
Leonard And Sandee

December 25, 1994

From

Loren And Anna Kendall

BOOKS BY DR. SCHULLER AVAILABLE IN THIS SPECIAL EDITION
Living Positively One Day at a Time
Love or Loneliness . . . You Decide
Reach Out for New Life
Your Future is Your Friend

Dr. Robert H. Schuller

Your Future Is Your Friend

An Inspirational Pilgrimage through the Twenty-third Psalm

The Cathedral Press
Garden Grove, California

Copyright © 1964 by Wm. B. Eerdmans Publishing Co.
Copyright © 1991 by Robert H. Schuller
All rights reserved under International and Pan-American
Copyright Conventions. No part of this book may be reproduced in
any form or by any electronic or mechanical means, including
information storage and retrieval systems, without permission in
writing from the publisher.

ISBN: 1-879989-01-8

Published by The Cathedral Press, Crystal Cathedral Ministries,
13280 Chapman Avenue, Garden Grove, California 92640.

The chapter entitled "A New Lease On Life" first appeared
in *The Christian Herald,* January 1963.
The author would also like to acknowledge the contributions
of Dorothy Poppen and Mildred Bartosh to the
original edition of this book.

Text design by Wanda Pfloog
Set in Sabon by Classic Typography

Printed in the United States of America

To Arvella
My Beloved Wife

To My New Readers

I am especially pleased that this book, along with several others, is again available. A number of members and friends of the Crystal Cathedral Ministries have indicated an interest in having them back in print and we are pleased that we were able to comply with their requests.

Since these books were first written and published, there have been many changes in the world and in our lives. Some of the wonderful people from whom I have learned are no longer with us. My children are now all grown and enrich our lives every day.

At first I thought I would revise these books but as our ministry continues to grow, finding the time to do so was almost impossible. Then I realized that revision wasn't really necessary — the references and illustrations are as valid as ever in calling our attention to the everlasting Gospel. I hope you will find this book a life-enriching and life-changing experience.

ROBERT SCHULLER

Contents

Preface

It is astonishing how people develop a tolerance for living. They learn to put up with life.

But what a profound pity, really. They tolerate life—they don't thrill to it. They endure life—they don't enjoy life. In spite of our affluence, life for too many people is an oppressive duty to be responsibly performed, an unwelcome chore to be carried out, a wearisome assignment they never asked for.

So existence is a dull, boring, monotonous affair. Even catastrophes are subconsciously welcomed as an exciting interlude in an otherwise boring existence. Not a few warmongers have managed to rally the masses behind them into a senseless, selfish war simply because the masses were bored and ripe and ready for some challenging change, hungry for a cause they could live and die for.

For many others life is a frightening experience. Early in life we discover the marriage of body and soul is a tenuous union, which will someday be swiftly, suddenly and severely severed. So we live out our existence under an unclearing cloud of despair, knowing not when the storm will break—and we will be dead!

For an inspiring, refreshing contrast we go back through the centuries to meet a stranger for whom life was obviously meaningful, exciting, and wonderful. His testimony has thrilled millions.

I am confident that if you will take a long, sincere, profound look at this man's faith you will discover his secret of glorious living; you will find that the experience of living can be an unfolding inspiration; somehow you'll have the strangely sweet feeling that *your future is your friend.*

ROBERT SCHULLER

The Lord is my shepherd; I shall not want.
He maketh me to lie down in green pastures:
he leadeth me beside the still waters.
He restoreth my soul:
he leadeth me in the paths of righteousness
for his name's sake.
Yea, though I walk through the valley
of the shadow of death,
I will fear no evil:
for thou art with me;
thy rod and thy staff they comfort me.
Thou preparest a table before me
in the presence of mine enemies:
thou anointest my head with oil;
my cup runneth over.
Surely goodness and mercy shallow follow me
all the days of my life:
and I will dwell in
the house of the Lord forever.

1

Start Living
a Full Life

One thing is certain: the half-full heart is a major reason for the moral decline in America today. Discontented people are dangerous people. Craving fulfillment, sensing we are missing out on something, we run madly after pleasure, eating, drinking, and swallowing pills until, overweight, drunk, and sexually wasted, we look with shame on ourselves, still suffering from an inner hunger we know not how to satisfy.

Are you hungry inside? Thirsty? Nothing satisfies that indefinable appetite? It is your instinctive craving for God!

I'm positive I have the answer for you!

"The Lord is my shepherd;
I shall not want. . . .
my cup runneth over."

IT'S UNBELIEVABLE that any man could feel so secure! And that in a day before Blue Cross, pension plans, social security, welfare-state programs, life insurance, penicillin, aspirins, insulin, blood plasma, or bottled oxygen! It casts quite a judgment on our insecure generation!

If ever there was a generation that needed to be born again it is this generation. This is the generation of the half-full cup. What a profound pity! One life to live, and we live it half-empty, and afraid!

W. H. Auden, the poet, visited a cocktail lounge on 42nd Street on Manhattan Island. He watched the lost souls come and go, sprawl over the bar, and stagger back to the lonely street. He scrawled these perceptive lines on a paper napkin:

Faces along the bar
Cling to their average day:

7

The light must never go out,
The music must always play, . . .
Lest we should see where we are,
Lost in a haunted wood,
Children afraid of the night
Who have never been happy or good.

Ours is a hungry generation. Nothing satisfies us. We are the insatiable society—empty. How can we analyze or describe the mood of our generation?

For millions, this emptiness takes the form of depression. The cup lacks luster, sparkle, zest, tang! We live out our days in a chronic state of depression. The prospect of our eventual death is a morbid thought. And the thought of a new tomorrow fails to stir our blood and thrill us. We are afraid to consider the thought of dying, and too depressed to contemplate the prospect of living. We do not know what depresses us more, the propsect of life or the prospect of death. A dilemma of despair!

For others the emptiness is anxiety. We have no happy expectations. Rather, we nurse a subconscious morbid mood, as if we intuitively suspect that something grave is about to befall us. Some are terribly concerned about the prospect of thermonuclear war, while others fear an irresponsible peace which would surrender our blood-bought freedom. And as though that were not enough, sociologists are causing us to suffer from claustrophobia—the fear that we live on a planet which is rapidly being overcrowded and overpopulated. We have the small-house feeling that too many uninvited people are planning to move in and live with us, including distant relatives with whom we do not agree and cannot get along. Unwelcome guests are forcing themselves upon our hesitant hospitality.

Still others would lay the blame for the disease of the half-filled cup on the technology of our day. It is an inevitable consequence of automation and mechanization. It is a result of collectivism and the lack of emphasis upon the individual. To illustrate:

> *The fellows up in personnel have a set of cards on*
> * me.*
> *The sprinkled perforations tell my individuality.*
> *And what am I? I am a chart upon the cards of IBM!*
> *The secret places of the heart have little secrecy to*
> * them.*
> *It matters now how I may work; how charged with*
> * punishments the scroll.*
> *The files are the masters of my fate: they are the cap-*
> * tains of my soul!*
> *Monday my brain began to buzz. I was in agony all*
> * night.*
> *I found out what the trouble was. They had my*
> * paper clip too tight.*

So, we lose our dignity. We have the uneasy feeling that were we to die tonight, nobody would miss us; and nobody would care.

Mark this as a certain fact: the half-full heart is a major reason for the moral decline in America today. Discontented people are dangerous people. Craving fulfillment, sensing we are missing out on something, we run madly after pleasure, eating, drinking, and swallowing pills until, overweight, drunk, and sexually wasted, we look with shame at ourselves, still suffering from an inner hunger we know not how to satisfy. The old anchorages have been cast aside and the moral boats are adrift in a sea of confusion.

Why is it so?

I went for a ride with my brother, a farmer in Iowa. Riding through the country, I saw a huge farm which I remembered as a child to be stately, dignified, beautiful with tall rows of green corn and golden acres of waving grain. Now that once proud farm is covered with acres of weeds, bent and dry and dead. Puzzled at the sad decline, I asked my brother why it was so and he said, "That farmer is in soil bank. The government pays him to raise nothing. It pays him to let his land lie idle."

But rich, fertile land will not be barren. Life churns with energy in ground that craves to create, that agonizes with a passion to produce until that rich soil, struggling against the tyranny of barrenness, rebels and shoots up weeds!

A human being is far greater than soil. We are born to create and produce. When our lives are not filled with a sense of creative purpose and we are frustrated in an effort to find meaning in life, we will produce weeds—divorce, drug addiction, alcoholism, and suicide.

We are sick! Do you know that Americans have more than three hundred billion dollars in the savings accounts? And the real estate of America is valued at more than one trillion dollars! Stroll further into the material realm. Polio has almost been eliminated. Billions of dollars of private money have been risked in research to produce for our benefit the miracle drugs. Today few are denied an education in the United States. But still the cup is half-empty!

How about you! Is your heart a bubble or a muscle? Does the slightest little problem prick your enthusiasm? The heart should be a strong, solid mass of red muscle. A muscle or a bubble—what kind of a heart do you have?

What is the answer? Did you hear about that fellow in Chicago, Illinois, who was suffering from this half-filled-cup disease? Something was lacking in his life and he didn't know what, so he went to a psychiatrist. The psychiatrist said that he was suffering from repressed sex desires and advised him to go out and have a good time. This Freudian adviser told him: "You are suffering from a guilt that is cruelly torturing you, inflicted upon you by an ignorant and medieval religion. Get wise and discover there is no god, there is no sin, there is no judgment, there is no hell, there is no punishment in the universe except as you punish yourself. Go out for goodness' sake and have a good time!" So he did. You know what happened? He became sicker than ever. Until, according to the account, he went back to the psychiatrist for a new appointment only to discover that the psychiatrist had committed suicide the week before! Practicing psychiatry without faith in God is like meeting a starving man in the desert and giving him a toothpick.

Is there no hope? That is the ultimate question. Is contentment in living just a cruel illusion? Is peace of mind a torturing mirage in the barren desert of life? Is it not possible for us to take our own life and fill it with love and laughter and joy? Well, all of the answers are uncertain, evasive, vacuous, until suddenly from the confusion of intellectual voices arises the voice of a man most convincing. He stands in the shadows. We cannot see who he is, nor can we discover his name. But his voice is strong! His heart is solid, red muscle! He does not preach. He does not condemn. His is no condescending testimony—just a simple strong voice of praise: "The Lord is my shepherd; I shall not want. He maketh me to lie down in green pastures: he leadeth me beside the still waters. he restoreth my soul . . . my cup runneth over." What marvelous confidence! And so convincing! What positive thinking!

His heart is full—full of courage, full of hope, full of joy!

How extraordinary! He doesn't brag about clever stock purchases, or the terrific real estate deal he pulled, or the V.I.P.'s he hobnobbed with at lunch. He is simply saying, "My cup is filled! I shall not want. I'm living a contented life!" (Reminds us of one who years later said, "I have learned in whatever state I find myself therewith to be content"!)

Who is this person? Who wrote this Psalm? David? Quite

11

possibly. Frankly, this is an assumption. True, David wrote many Psalms and he himself was a shepherd lad. But for all we know, the author of this Psalm may have been an old man who had lost his wife and the last of his children and wrote this testimony of faith.

Or was this author a blind beggar sitting at the side of the road who, though poor in body and in spirit, had found God and lived with hope in his heart? Who knows, he may have been a leper—a leper ready to die! A leper with only stumps of hands and facing the end, because he writes, "Yea, though I walk through the valley of the shadow of death, I will fear no evil: for though art with me."

We do not know his name, but we do know his secret! What is his secret? Is it escape from sickness, trouble, difficulty? Hardly. Enemies surround him. Death licks at his heels. It sounds like he is living all alone.

What is his secret? It is his way of thinking. There is no negative thinking here. You know what saps energy, joy, and enthusiasm out of your heart and life? What drains the sparkle out of life and leaves you depressed? It is self-pity! The vitality-sapping ideas that you have been cheated or abandoned, or deserted by God and your friends. This is what drains life! And it is greed and resentment or hate and suspicion or distrust and cynicism or guilt—a feeling that you have done something wrong and you cannot die tonight and meet God with confidence!

Ah, here is the secret! No, it is not morbid. It is majestic, when you think of it. The secret of this man's greatness, and courage, and fullness of heart is that he knows he is a child of God and he can live or die without fear.

It is a well-established fact that the underlying cause of all fear and anxiety is the fear of death. *This man is ready to die!* He can meet death with dignity! Morris West in his novel *The Devil's Advocate* tells the story of a priest who, in the strong years of his life, goes to the doctor and is told that he has an incurable cancer which will take his life in a matter of months. He leaves the doctor's office. He goes for a walk through the park. He hears the birds singing, sees flowers and trees, watches children at play, lovers on a bench, old men leaning on their canes. Suddenly a terrifying thought invades his mind: he is not prepared to die! And a terrible wave of terror sweeps over him.

But in this Twenty-Third Psalm we meet a man who has surrendered his life to God and he finds real security!

How can you acquire this security, the confidence that your life is under the wings of a redeeming, restoring, reinforcing God? How can you get it?

Once there was a blind man. He was named Bartimaeus. He was sitting on the side of the dry, dusty road in Palestine. I can see him in a soiled white robe that covers all of his body save the sun-tanned, calloused, bare feet. His face is raw leather, tawny, tough, lined. His thin, bony-fingered hands are mapped with bulging blood vessels that run like ridges over the surface through forests of wiry hair. His dusty eyes are closed. Flies crawl over his eyes and through his beard. There is dust and dirt in his hair from sleeping in the ditches at night. And all he holds in his hand is an almost empty cup with a dented coin. He rattles it when he hears somebody come down the road. Blind Bartimaeus—what a pitiful specimen of humanity! And then in the distance his keen ears, grown more sensitive because of his blindness, hear the shuffle of many feet and the rising swell of a chorus of voices. As the crowd moves closer to him, he hears someone drop the name, "Jesus of Nazareth." Jesus of Nazareth? There are those, he remembers, who claim that this Jesus performs miracles. On an impulse he cries out, "Jesus, Son of David, have mercy on me!" And Jesus stops, and heals him!

Now back to ourselves in this jet-age America. Are you searching for faith? Then, cry out, "Christ, have mercy on me!" It is the one prayer that God always answers. But you say,

13

"I am a Christian and I go to church, but my cup is still only half-full! I am not living a full life! How about me?"

Let me answer that with a story from Joseph Meyer, who for years has played the part of Christ in the passion play in South Dakota. He carries the cross and speaks the words. He told this story to Marcus Bach: "One day the crowds were getting smaller and smaller. Nothing seemed right and nothing seemed good. I was carrying the cross through a performance of the play to a small group of people and I was repeating my lines most accurately: 'Why take ye thought for the morrow. Sufficient unto the day is the evil thereof, oh ye of little faith.'" Then he confessed, "In my mind I thought, 'Joseph Meyer, you don't believe it. You are just saying it! Joseph Meyer, *stop saying it and start believing it.*'" He added, "I thereupon determined in my intellectual will that I was going to believe it. Things have never been the same since." If you are a Christian, stop saying it and start believing it!

Are you hungry? Thirsty? Nothing satisfies? It is your instinctive craving for God! Allow me a final plea. I am positive I have the answer for you! Give me a chance to prove it. There are three philosophies of life. (1) "What's mine is mine; I'm going to keep it." This is selfishness. It will make you miserable. (2) "What's yours is mine; I'm going to get it." This is greed. It will drain you of all joy. (3) "What's mine is yours too; I want to share it." This is Christianity! It makes you feel good when you are good to those around you, and it makes you feel God-like when you are generous to those who don't expect it and don't deserve it! God comes into your life when you give yourself away to Him and humanity in loving service.

Want evidence? Consider Christ! What a full life He lived! Full of faith, joy, purpose, peace, and power. Why? Eternity was His friend! That's one reason. And He lived to love and serve. He was always busy giving Himself away. While His blood was dripping, someone said: "He saved others—himself he cannot save." Quite true! If you want to fill your life you have to pour it out! *Involvement is the only indulgence that really satisfies!*

A final witness, to prove this point. Dr. Louis Evans tells of visiting a mission station in Korea. A medical missionary friend invited him to witness a major operation. The surgical ward was a crude shop. The heat was stifling. The odors almost overwhelmed the visiting American minister. But the steady missionary doctor kept at his task with untiring skill. After seven hours he stood up, faced Dr. Evans, and announced that the job was done. They walked back to the modest office and Dr. Evans asked the missionary, "How much would you have been paid for that operation in America?" "Probably, five hundred dollars," the doctor answered. Evans said, "I'm curious. How much do you get here in Korea in this mission station?" The doctor picked from his desk a dented copper coin and said, "Well, to begin with—this. She came into our mission holding this coin and with tears in her eyes asked me, 'Doctor, do you suppose this would pay for an operation?' I looked at her and said, 'I think so!'" He went on, "To begin with—this dented coin, but most of all"—and tears filled his eyes—"most of all it makes me feel so good inside knowing that my hands for a few hours have been the hands of Jesus Christ healing a sick woman."

This is the answer.

This is the way.

It means that you, too, must come to Christ and invite Him to come into your life. If you do, He will fill you full. One of those who knew Him best tried it and left ths triumphant testimony: "And of his fulness have we all received, grace for grace."

2

A New Lease
On Life

Today, if there are birds winging and you do not see them, children singing and you do not hear them, flowers blooming and you do not enjoy them, God moving and you do not feel Him—keep waiting, keep praying. God will not mock your waiting. God will not laugh at your praying, God will not be deaf to your pleading. Suddenly you hear footsteps in the hall and your prison door swings open, and you are free again!

"He restoreth my soul . . ."

IF I WERE TO write my own text for this chapter it would be, "If you then, being evil, know how to restore old automobiles, ancient art treasures, oil paintings of the masters, and priceless antiques, how much more shall your Father who is in heaven restore your soul after it has suffered scars and bruises in life's pilgrimage!"

We had quite an experience this summer in our vacation cottage. We experienced a terrifying storm. Writhing, turbulent clouds, bull-whipped by white streaks of lightning, stampeded by crashes of thunder, rumbled across the sky. Trees, tortured by cruel winds, screamed with pain. Their dismembered limbs fell bleeding to the ground. The tender earth, ancient friend of the elm and oak, groaned in sympathy, helpless to relieve the suffering trees.

Then, suddenly, as if an answer to a grand command from outer space, the renegade storm clouds began to break up, scatter, and flee like hoodlums racing from the streets, back to their forbidding alleys. And the bright stars came out to laugh again, like little children returning once more to safe streets for happy play. The sky cleared. The stars, washed clean, sparkled again. And from the east a huge yellow moon sailed calm and serene through the soundless sea of space. Peace was restored.

"He restoreth my soul." This is God's way of saying that after the storm there will come renewed calm.

Can you remember a night when you could not sleep? It seemed the day would never dawn. You finally rose from a bed that refused to give you comfort or rest. You walked out into the still black morning. You looked anxiously for the first stirring of creeping daylight but the morning star was still sleeping under the blanket of night. Around you an unlighted world huddled in the chilly shadows. Would daylight never come?

And then, out of the silent shadows, you heard a single note—the sweet, fresh, wide-awake note of a bird! And after a pause another note from another corner answered. The birds stirred. Note answered note. Song answered song until the wakening birds made the morning happy with music, as if singing a processional for the royal sun about to make its gallant entrance over the eastern hill. And the born-again morning finally came. Daylight was restored.

"He restoreth my soul." It is God's way of promising us that after a fitful night there will be a new day; after the storm, new calmness; after the night, a new day; and after the winter, a resurrected springtime.

I never fail to remind new Christians who join our church that there are seasons in the spiritual life. For most people the beginning of the Christian life is a springtime experience. The icy sea of doubt is broken; a new life springs from a cold heart. No wonder people describe it by saying, "I've been born again!" This is the springtime season of the soul. When the Christian matures through the disciplines, there is growth, sometimes

20

painful, in exposure to summer sun and wind, and finally the ripening of the fruit. The harvest season arrives and you offer to God the fruit of a life of service. And, strangely, it is usually after a period of fruitful service that the wintertime comes.

It is the shock of it that bothers us most. We never thought we would see those old doubts, those old sins, those old troubles again! But here they are back, knocking at the door once more. The shock of it—and the loneliness of it—is what disturbs us. Secretly we suspect that we alone are going through this wintry season.

The truth is that every Christian passes through a wintertime in his spiritual pilgrimage. Arthur Gordon, telling the story of Norman Vincent Peale, paints a dramatic picture of the time when Norman Peale went through this winter season in a London garden. But his "soul was restored" in a great new religious experience! And Catherine Marshall, in the biography of her husband Peter, tells us that there was a time when her great preacher husband came to her and said, "Catherine, what's the use! My prayers don't get above the top of my head."

There are times when the light flickers, the glow burns low, the zeal fades, desolateness sweeps over the soul, doubt flashes its frigid face across our wintry path. Music no longer stirs the heart. Worship no longer lifts the spirit. Sweet tears no longer come to visit the eye. Prayer—a foolish empty wind! The heart shivers in a cold cell of cynicism. The knife has lost its keen edge. The trumpet tone is flat. The window, once clean and sparkling, is covered with film. And you wonder whether you still love your wife, whether you still believe in God, and whether or not you are in the right profession.

Careful! This is the winter season of the soul! Make no rash, impulsive, far-reaching decisions. This is a dark night for the heart. This is a stormy season for your spirit. And wintertime can be so lonely, so cold, so barren, so uninspiring and so long!

Why do these seasons come? Sometimes I suspect through simple neglect. Carelessly we skip a church service, we neglect

21

our daily devotions, we are too busy to read our Bible and pray, and we foolishly think we are none the worse because of our undisciplined spiritual life. I can neglect to water and feed the plants in my garden and they seem none the worse for it until, suddenly, one day I discover that they are withering in the sun! G. K. Chesterton once confessed that when he was a young man he decided to put "his religion in the drawer for a while and have a good time." He would remember where he had put it and when he was in the mood for it, he would go back and reclaim it. Years later he went back for it. He opened the drawer, but it was empty! Dry seasons are inevitable if we neglect the spiritual exercises. The only way to keep your religion is to keep using it.

Accumulated blows of misfortune can suddenly cause our faith to freeze over for a season. One of the great Christian ministers of the twentieth century was the late Dr. John Baillie. His mother lost her first husband while she was still young and childless. Her second husband was the Rev. Baillie, a minister in the highlands of Scotland. Into this marriage and manse were born three sons, John, Donald, and Peter. But John, the oldest, was only five when his preacher father died. Mrs. Baillie, now twice widowed, took her three sons and moved close to a university town. Of course she had a plan. She was determined to put her three sons through the university of Edinburgh. And she did. She worked and struggled and prayed and believed — and succeeded. It was 1914. Now John and Donald were graduate ministers of high esteem. Her son Peter had graduated from medical school. He announced that he would become a medical missionary and sailed for India. For Mrs. Baillie this was the high time of her life. It seemed as if all of the years of struggle were suddenly worth while. Then came the tragic blow. Peter, still in language school in India, died in a drowning accident before he could begin his missionary work. A biographer, John Baillie's wife, reports, "This shattered Mrs. Baillie." Strong and great saint that she was, this tragedy was too much for her. It broke her. But then the biographer writes, "Her sons John and Donald tenderly nursed her back to a merciful faith in a wonderful Providence." Her soul was restored!

And sometimes a secret sin harbored in the heart is enough to cause our soul and our spiritual life to become barren and dry, just as a grain of sand in the gas line of a car causes power to fail. If there is spiritual power lost in your life, check your secret heart carefully.

What shall we do when the shivering season strikes the soul? Jesus gave a beautiful answer in a parable, "Ye ought always to pray and faint not." Like the widow who kept appealing to the judge, refusing to take no for an answer, so we, too, must unceasingly pray to God. "I will not let Thee go, O Lord, except Thou bless me."

But there is a right way and a wrong way to pray.

G. Studdert Kennedy tells of a moment in his wartime experience when the battle seemed as if it would go on for eternity. "The bombardment lasted for over two hours. We could do nothing except sit still and wait. The sergeant on one side of me swore a great oath and made jokes by turn. A man somewhere on the other side kept praying aloud, in an unbroken and despairing kind of way, shivering out piteous supplications to God for protection and safety. I wish that chap would chuck that praying. It turns me sick . . . it is disgusting somehow. It isn't religion, it is cowardice. It isn't prayer, it is wind . . . I wouldn't mind if he would pray for pluck, but it is all for safety . . . "

By contrast we think of another Soldier entrenched in his olive-tree battlefield who was overheard praying, "Father, all things are possible with thee. Let this cup pass from me. Nevertheless not my will but thine be done."

I hear a cynic coming along who says, "Little good that praying did. Look at the cross!" And I remind the impulsive cynic that he judges too hastily. For three days later it was Easter morning! What were the first unspoken thoughts that entered into the mind of Jesus when He walked out of the prison tomb that crisp, holy Easter morning? Did he look the happy sun full in its face and secretly say, "He restoreth my soul"?

True prayer will bring renewal.

Pray — and wait! *Wait* — this is the painful but powerpacked word. Somewhere John Henry Jowett has reminded us that "God gives us the grace to move ahead, to back up, to stand up, and also to sit still and wait." "Wait on the Lord . . . and he shall strengthen thine heart: wait, I say, on the Lord." Have you prayed and there is no change? Then turn your face to the east, your thoughts to springtime, and your heart to God, and wait.

"How long must I wait?" you ask. Greater saints than you have asked that question. The patience of God is terrifying. The slowness of His providence is torturing. For we are still very childish in our concept of time. A year seems like an age to a young man. We must mature like old men — when a year does not seem long any more.

How long? The Psalmist asked: "Return, O Lord, how long?" Isaiah as well as that discouraged prophet Jeremiah raised the question. And when Jeremiah realized that the battle would be longer than expected he wisely advised, "This captivity is long, build ye houses!" For some of us our battle is going to be long. Begin digging and laying spiritual foundations, and build a house of faith and prayer or you will never be able to stick it out! *God has never promised that He would hurry up!*

There is a passage at the opening of the Agamemnon of Aeschylus. A lonely watchman crouches in the damp night on the roof of the palace. Night after night, month after month, he scans the dark sky, waiting for the gleam of the bonfire that shall announce the fall of Troy and the ending of the Trojan War. Suddenly, one night like all the others, he sees the flames leaping jubilantly into the sky. Now the watchman, his long vigil over, leaps to his feet and cries out, "All hail, thou light in darkness, harbinger of day!"

Listen, Christian, wait and pray and keep looking for the sunrise. God will surely send you a fresh blessing.

For ours is a wait—not a wake. Sisera was slain in battle. His mother, not knowing his fate, waited at her lattice window for her son to come home. She raised the pitiful question, "Why is his chariot so long in coming?" For her this was a wake—not a wait. It reminds us of the man whose whole life is lived out without God. Aged, with no pride behind and no hope ahead, he waits in vain for some of the joys of life to be restored—a tragic wake.

Not so for the man whose life has been a walk with God. He may encounter barren times, but he waits upon the Lord for a fresh blessing. And his last years are his best.

Does God seem far from you today? Wait and pray. God will visit you again! "His going forth shall be as sure as the morning."

Why am I so sure? Because God has promised this. "Say to them that are of a fearful heart, Be strong, fear not: behold, your God will come with vengeance, even God with a recompence; he will come and save you . . . In the wilderness shall waters break out, and streams in the desert. . . . And the ransomed of the Lord shall return . . . with songs and everlastingly joy upon their heads: they shall obtain joy and gladness, sorrow and sighing shall flee away" (Isaiah 35).

"I waited patiently for the Lord. He inclined unto me and heard me cry. He lifted me up out of the pit and put my feet upon a rock. He established my goings and put a new song in my heart, even praise unto my God" is the testimony of another saint.

I write this out of deep personal experience. I remember a wintertime in my spiritual life. I have never doubted my love for God or my faith in Christ. But I have passed through seasons when I wondered about my calling. Did God want me to continue to preach the gospel all my life? Perhaps He had a better man in mind to take my place. Until one morning, alone in my quiet room, God visited me. I was overcome with the joy of it. I was overpowered with a desire to preach and reassured that the Holy Spirit would make me adequate to the responsibility. I went to my wife in the kitchen and through my tears I told her, God has called me again, and on my thirty-seventh birthday, too!"

Giacomo Nerone, candidate for sainthood in *The Devil's Advocate,* asks, "How does one come back to belief out of unbelief? Out of sin, it is easy; an act of repentance. An errant child returns to a Father because the Father is still there. But in unbelief there is no Father. . . . Did he love me or had He forgotten me forever? This was the real terror . . . as I look back on it now from the security I have reached I tremble and sweat and pray desperately: Hold me close. Never let me go again. Never hide Your face from me. It is terrible in the dark! . . . How did I come to Him? He alone knows. I groped for Him and could not find Him. I prayed to Him unknown and He did not answer. I wept at night for the loss of Him. . . . Then one day He was there again!"

How about you? Do you feel your spiritual life has lost its luster? Has your religion lost its reality? Are prayer, God, Christ, unreal?

Today, if there are birds winging and you do not see them, children singing and you do not hear them, flowers blooming and you do not enjoy them, God moving and you do not feel Him—keep waiting, keep praying! God will not mock your waiting. God will not laugh at your praying. God will not be deaf to your pleading. Suddenly you hear footsteps in the hall and your prison door swings open, and you are free again!

"Sometimes a light surprises a Christian while he sings! It is the Lord who comes with healing on His wings." Restored! And there is a new bloom on the rose, a sharp edge on the knife; trumpet tones are clear again; the enemy raises a white

26

flag, crocuses bloom through the snow; streams break out in the desert; the moon sails calm again as God returns to the waiting heart!

You rejoice! Your hallelujah has returned to your heart! "They that wait upon the Lord shall renew their strength, they shall mount up with wings like eagles. . . . they shall run and not faint!" Amen, Amen, and Hallelujah!

3

Trouble
Isn't Always
Trouble

But the voice of God is overpowed by the roar of the traffic on the freeway, the moan of ambulances, the wail of sirens, the growl of buses, the rude interruption of the doorbell. Jet airplanes, two-ton diesel trucks, trains, television, telephones fill our everyday world with noises the ears were never designed to tolerate. An irritating assortment of unnatural sounds drown out the silver-soft voice of God that whispers through the pines, and speaks through foaming waves that swish on salty sand, "Lie down, my child, and rest awhile. Take a break from the freeway form of living. Your nerves weren't made to stand the strain, your body wasn't engineered for such stress, and your eyes can't stand some of the temptations!"

But we refuse to lie down until God makes us lie down!

"He maketh me to lie down . . . "

IT IS THE PSALMIST'S shocking honesty that makes us trust him—he is so brutally frank! He openly admits that sometimes the shepherd forcibly takes the sheep from their field of play and food, and makes them lie down—"He maketh me to lie down in green pastures." Which is his way of saying that trouble is not always trouble!

And what is trouble, you ask! You could get a variety of answers to that question. Trouble is a flat tire on the freeway when you are late for an urgent appointment; or your little girl makes her last clean dress dirty just when you are ready to leave; or it is running out of money when you're away from home—or simply running out of money at home! Trouble is final exams when you haven't finished the textbook; or remembering today an important appointment you forgot yesterday; or finding yourself without a comb, hair disheveled, and important people waiting to see you; or trouble is running out of gas on a long lonely road at night in strange mountains. And trouble is many things far worse than any of these! Of course, there is such a thing as trouble!

But it is obvious that in our pitiful judgments we often label as troubles what in time and truth are really blessings in disguise. Mysteries of Providence we should call them.

I am indebted to a wonderful old Christian who was past ninety when confined to a bed. "I see you are having a little trouble," I sympathized. The smile wrinkles in her face cracked and she chided me, "Oh, no, I'm not having trouble. I just didn't know when to quit and the good Lord made me lie down. But I have been having a wonderful time reading His Word, and talking with Him at night when I couldn't sleep, and He turns this bed into a green pasture. 'He maketh me to lie down in green pastures.'"

This reminds me of my children who love to play too long, too hard and too late into the night, until their mother or father comes and makes them lie down on a bed they do not welcome. And later, while they sleep soundly, we slip back into the room on quiet feet to see tranquil faces floating on soft pillows.

Now we all know that most of us adults in America are living too fast, too hard, and too strenuously. We are caught in a bumper-to-bumper way of living. We are always on the move—driving, going, just coming home, or just getting ready to go out—but always on the move, so that we hardly know how to relax for a quiet evening at home without taking something from a box or a bottle to unwind us. We are restless, nervous, fidgety. Even when we are relaxing, we have an almost guilty feeling that we should be doing something, or going somewhere!

All the while God is trying to say something: "Slow down and start living. Enjoy your friends, your family and your faith!" But the voice of God is overpowered by the roar of the traffic on the freeway, the moan of ambulances, the wail of sirens, the growl of buses, the rude interruption of the door-bell. Jet airplanes, two-ton diesel trucks, trains, television, tele-phones fill our everyday world with noises the ears were never designed to tolerate. An irritating assortment of unnatural sounds drown out the silver-soft voice of God that whispers through the pines, and speaks through foaming waves that swish on salty sand, "Lie down, my child, and rest awhile. Take a break from the freeway form of living. Your nerves weren't made to stand the strain, your body wasn't engineered for such stress, and your eyes can't stand some of the tempta-tions!"

But we refuse to lie down until God makes us lie down! And then, miserable victims of self-pity, we think that we are in trouble!

Oh, be slow to judge, my soul! Is it really trouble? Or is it a divinely disguised blessing? That sickness, that lost job, that unfaithful friend, that financial loss—be not swift to label it a wolf at the door. It may be a sheep in wolf's clothing!

Is the grinding wheel that puts a fresh edge on the knife, or the hoe that breaks up hard soil and plows out weeds, or the sharp knife of the gardener that prunes and snips useless growth to give greater strength to the roots and the trunk, or the north wind that forces the pine to send down roots of steel into granite earth, or the rod in the shepherd's hand that strikes the sheep lest it run blindly off a precipice, or the surgeon's bloody scalpel that cuts away the foreign tumor, or the sculp-tor's hard hammer and brutal chisel that chip and polish—are these not all our friends? The chisel, the hammer, the scalpel, the rod, the wind, the knife, the hoe, the wheel, are these not our friends?

Trouble is not always trouble! It is often God's way of mak-ing us lie down, turn around, sit still, pray, work harder, or start over again!

When is trouble not trouble, you ask? When it protects you from an unknown hazard on the road ahead, or shelters you from a sin that, unknown to you, lurks furtively in your path waiting to tempt and trip you, then trouble is not trouble!

When trouble cleans up collected clutter that you valued too highly and did not have the courage to discard or destroy, or when it tears out of your life an unworthy friend whom you were unable to help and who was not a good influence on your life, then trouble is not trouble!

When trouble makes you furious enough to fight for a good cause you were too busy to serve, or frustrates you so that you quit a job that was too long hiding your real talents and forces you to discover new skills and hidden talents that were lying undetected like veins of gold under cabbage fields, then trouble is not trouble!

When trouble causes two parties, long unspeaking, to bury the hatchet; when it makes a person forget himself and start thinking of others; when it makes a greedy man generous, a hard man compassionate, a cold heart warm, a thoughtless man considerate—then trouble is not without its reward!

When trouble teaches you valuable lessons that you would have been too blind to see, too arrogant to believe, or too stubborn to accept any other way than by this bed of pain; when it slams a door in your face to force you out of a rut that you would never have had the courage to leave and leads you down a new road through an open door, then trouble may be a most valuable experience!

When trouble stirs up gratitude for gifts you have taken too long for granted, or creates an opportunity for you to think, read, write, pray, then trouble is really a friend who comes to your door wearing your enemy's jacket!

So often trouble is only a part of the painful growing process, like a seed buried alive by a seemingly merciless fate under suffocating ground in a windowless grave, until in supreme agony it ruptures into new life! This death, burial, pain, is not trouble! It is the travail of new birth! "Except a grain of wheat fall into the ground and die, it abideth alone."

When trouble breaks your heart and makes your knees buckle, and forces penitent tears from eyes sealed in prayer to Almighty God, then trouble may turn out to be the redeeming agony before new birth!

Just what kind of people do you think we would be if we never had any trouble? For we build hard muscles in heart and body when we lift heavy loads. Tough times make calluses that may someday save our hands from bleeding! How right is Holy Writ, "Whom the Lord loveth he chasteneth."

Truly, we learn courage when we face danger, we learn patience when we endure suffering, we learn tenderness when we taste pain, we learn to prize true friends when false ones forsake us, we treasure health when illness strikes, and we learn to prize freedom when we are in danger of losing it! Without trouble we would be like plants that have sprouted, grown, and nurtured in the overprotected shelter of a hothouse, too tender ever to live in the open!

We have matured as Christians when we learn that there is no progress without pain, there is no conversion without crisis, there is no birth without painful travail, there is no salvation without agonizing repentance, and no Easter without a Good Friday! There is no service without suffering. What good would an ox be if it refused to wear a yoke?

So you are having trouble? You feel cheated and abandoned by God? Remember, "The eagle stirreth up her nest in order that the young might learn to fly!" Your trouble may be your great opportunity!

Go down to the beach and watch the mountainous waves come crashing in and you will see two ways to meet a wave. The frightened, timid soul sees the monster wave looming, mounting, threatening. He turns, stumbling through the foamy shallows, and being too slow, he is overtaken, upset, flattened and sent sputtering in the surf by the liquid mountain. But farther in the deep you see a skillful rider of the surf who watches carefully the wave as it builds, swells, rises; and instead of running from the wave, he rides it! Instead of being flattened, he is lifted! Instead of being made low, he is raised high and carried far!

Every trouble has vast built-in opportunities to grow, to learn, to serve, or to be cleansed. Imagination can turn your bed of trouble into fruitful pasture. Your time of lying low can be your morning of spiritual refreshment.

Whatever you do, don't make the mistake of thinking that your neighbor, with his seemingly untroubled life, is having all the good fortune! While your trouble may be blessing in disguise, his blessing may be trouble in hiding! Success has spoiled many a man. Security can stifle initiative and ambition. Prestige leads too quickly to pride. Power corrupts. Wealth brings with it vast temptations. Prosperity has more perils than poverty. I remember a magazine article by a famous actress, entitled, "My Beauty Was My Downfall." She later committed suicide. Why, that neighbor you envy for her untroubled life may be sick with boredom!

What must you do with your trouble? Sir Harry Lauder, a great Scottish comedian, received the tragic news that his son was killed in the First World War. He wrote these penetrating lines: "In a time like this there are three courses open to a man. He may give way to despair, sour upon the world, and become a grouch. He may endeavor to drown his sorrow in drink or in a life of waywardness and wickedness . . . or he may turn to God!"

These are the three choices open to you.

If you use your head, there is only one choice that makes any sense. Turn to God! Years later you will testify that once you were stopped in your tracks by what appeared to be an impossibly cruel mountain that blocked your path. You were mercilessly forced to climb it with bleeding hands and a breaking heart, until you reached the summit and there you found, hidden behind the rugged peak, the greenest little pasture encircling a heaven-pure mountain lake! The greenest pastures I have seen have been in the terrible mountain ranges—precious pockets painfully gouged out by grinding glaciers centuries before.

Let your troubles lead you to Christ and they will prove to be the best friends you ever had!

4

A Promise of Victory
When Defeat
Seems Certain

The Christian walks the streets of this world like a chaste young girl walking alone at night on a dark street in a dangerous part of town where an enemy lurks to despoil her beauty. The world waits to seduce, and if that fails, to buy, and if that fails—to rape! It is true, we are surrounded by enemies—doubt, resentment, jealousy, pride, self-pity, and lust. How can we win?

*"Thou preparest a table before me
in the presence of mine enemies . . . "*

THERE ARE TIMES when a Christian is like a kernel of corn
lying in the barnyard, where a flock of hungry chickens
scratch the ground in search of food. The lot of a Christian
is sometimes as dangerous as is the lot of a lost lamb caught
in a thicket with a pack of wolves drawing closer and closer—
until a straight-backed, firm-necked, brave-eyed shepherd,
holding a menacing staff in white-knuckled hands, comes to the
rescue. He lifts the lamb to his bosom, brandishes high his
threatening rod, and the wolves flee. Which reminds us of Jesus
who centuries ago said, "I am the good shepherd . . . I know
my sheep . . . no man will pluck them out of my hand . . . I
will lay down my life for my sheep." And He did!

We hear the dull thud of hammer blows. Suddenly there
appears on the country skyline just outside the city of Jerusalem a cross and on it a man hangs from dripping hands.

Only a few hours before in the night Jesus had met with

41

his twelve disciples. The scene was an upper room somewhere in the city of hate. Christ celebrated the Passover and established the Holy Communion. As He broke the bread, He said, "This is my body . . . do this in remembrance of me." Even then, as He sat at the table, He was surrounded by enemies lurking in the night. Somewhere in the city were Annas and Caiaphas, and Judas running on hot heels to collect his loot of thirty pieces of silver, thinking how easy it was to make this money—thirty pieces for kissing this man! Here we see a table prepared in the presence of enemies. For in this wild city we find Pontius Pilate, soldiers with hammers, demented religious leaders, and thousands of people whose lives are so empty that they would enjoy a crucifixion (like some people enjoy a bull fight: blood is better than boredom).

During that dramatic sight, while enemies surround them, Jesus and the disciples of our Lord sit at a table to eat the broken bread and drink the juice of grapes. "Thou preparest a table before me in the presence of mine enemies." "This do," He said, "in remembrance of me."

Astounding! This was the way Christ wanted to be remembered. He left no library of authoritative books, no sculptored monuments of stone, no shrine at His birth place or burial place, and no portrait of His face—only this ceremony. Why this? Is it God's dramatic way of reminding His redeemed children that we can be assured of victory when defeat surrounds us? The Holy Communion is God preparing a table before us in the presence of our enemies.

Make no mistake about it—as Christians we are surrounded by enemies! We are Christians in a pagan world! Not long ago I sat in a meeting and listened to a prominent psychologist who declared that Moses was a schizophrenic, that the Bible is a completely discredited book, that God does not exist, and, to cap his demonic lecture, he blasphemed the name of Jesus—and the crowd applauded! This was the first experience in my life when I really felt that I was surrounded by enemies. It is seldom that obvious!

But we must always remember that as Christians we are surrounded by a sinful world bent on destroying God in any form. And if God appears in your life, be sure that the sinful forces of this world will spare no effort to destroy the image of God within you. Usually the enemy is so subtle that we do not sense the danger.

While attending a meeting in the United Nations building very recently, dining in the delegates' room, it was difficult for me to imagine that among these men there were the hard-core international Communists who would not stop at murder if they felt it would be a quicker and more successful way to win the world struggle. It was quite impossible to imagine that behind the gray flannel suit, the neat white shirt, the Windsor tie, and the placid, disarming smiles were the souls of men who held only contempt for the Christian philosophy of life.

Perhaps our greatest danger is that we are not aware of the peril. There are times in our lives when we do not feel the vile breath of the enemy hot on our back. The world looks so friendly; we feel no need for prayer; the enemy has apparently fled. But watch out! This is only a dangerous peace offensive. This is not the warm wind of spring but a cruelly disarming wind of winter. A tender wind in January may tragically deceive the trees and cause them to send out premature buds with great energy. Suddenly, however, the wind blows cold again, and the shivering trees, unable to cover their tender young buds, freeze in the returning winter storm. The bulging buds die and the trees mourn the loss of their stillborn. The enemy is around us and the enemy is sin! "I send you forth as sheep in the midst of wolves," Jesus said.

The Christian walks the streets of this world like a chaste young girl walking alone at night on a dark street in a dangerous part of town where an enemy lurks to despoil her beauty.

43

The world waits to seduce, and if that fails, to buy, and if that fails—to rape! The simile is not extreme. It is true. We are surrounded by enemies—The enemies may be doubt, resentment, jealousy, pride, self-pity, and lust. But enemies they are.

How can we win? Does the taking of Holy Communion help? Is the Lord's table a promise of victory in the presence of enemies? Yes!

But how can taking Communion help us? The key word is "remember." "This do in remembrance of me." These words are found on communion tables around the world—painted in gold leaf on polished walnut, gracefully carved in oak, chiseled in stone, and burned in steel!

How can memory give us inner power and strength? In the first place, the Christian is motivated to victorious living when he remembers that God will stop at nothing to help us. When a Christian eats the broken bread and drinks the wine at Holy Communion he is remembering that God went to the utter limits to redeem us from sin. Again and again I am asked why Christianity uses the cross as its symbol. Is this not a morbid symbol? On the contrary! The cross is an inspiring reminder that God will stop at nothing to save His children.

Why did God have to resort to a cross to redeem men? The answer is obvious if we think about it seriously. Sweet words alone do not redeem men. After Christ delivered the beautiful sermon on the mount men crucified Him! Sweet words may impress people—but only sacrificial love wins disciples! "Love so amazing, so divine, demands my life, my soul, my all." "I, if I be lifted up, will draw all men unto myself" was the prophecy of Jesus Christ. He uttered the most beautiful words ever spoken by a human being; He performed miracles of compassionate healing that have never been equalled; He lived a humble life of devoted service to men of all races and classes, but *this was not enough!* In the final analysis it would only be through His own self-sacrifice that men would be drawn in complete commitment to His cause.

44

But why a cross? How we would welcome an easier way! That is because we think small. Our ideas, at best, would be ludicrous, like the general who suggested a plan to the United States Air Force for knocking down enemy bombers. He suggested that fighter planes drag long chains behind them and fly over the bombers until the hanging chains would foul up the propellers and the bombers would fall!

God cannot promiscuously forgive and irresponsibly overlook evil. Sin must be punished. God is a moral Being. And the cross was God's way of atoning for our sins and redeeming our souls. So the Christian comes to Holy Communion and is motivated to victorious living by the memory that God has stopped at nothing to make our victory over sin possible.

Holy Communion also reminds us that we are redeemed children of God. Are you facing an implacable foe, Christian? Never despair! During the French Revolution Louis XVI was beheaded, then Marie Antoinette, and finally they brought out the little dauphin, the heir to the throne, who was to become Louis XVII. The mob shouted, "To the guillotine with the prince! An end to kings!" Then someone conceived of a more diabolical scheme. "Don't kill him. Death will only send his soul to heaven. Hand him over to old Meg. She is the most wicked woman in Paris. Let her teach him filth. Let her teach him to sin. Then his soul will go to hell too!" According to some legends, the prince was turned over to old Meg. She dressed him in rags and tried to teach him to lie, swear and steal. But again and again when old Meg tried to teach him a vile word he would clench his little princely fist, stamp his feet, and shout, "I will not say it! I will not say it! I was born to be a king, and I will not say it!" Holy Communion reminds us who we are. We are children of the King! When we leave the table with head high, proud that we are God's children, our strengthened dignity dispels the cheap temptations of sin.

And Holy Communion reminds us that God is on our side in the battle. Winston Churchill first met Major General Claire

Chennault at Quebec. The British Prime Minister saw the square-jawed officer sitting in the room and whispered to his aide, "Who is that man?" The aide replied, "That's Claire Chennault, the flying tiger of China." Then Churchill replied, "What a face! What a face! Thank God, he's on our side!" Christian, look down in the glass that holds the shimmering wine at Holy Communion and see reflected in this crimson mirror the face of Jesus Christ, and rejoice that He is on your side. The widow of the flying tiger once remarked, "When I was with him, nothing seemed impossible." How much more can the Christian say that nothing is impossible when he is close to God.

Frequently I fly from Los Angeles to New York. The commercial flights jet westward out of Kennedy International Airport, soar over the Pacific, and make a sweeping curve over Catalina Island. Catalina is a lonely island surrounded by an ancient, unloving sea. For centuries this fathomless ocean, which is really not pacific, has sent its merciless waves crashing over this stubborn island. One might suspect that someday this desolate outpost would crumble and disappear into the deep. But I am sure it will last till the end of time. For it is granite-rooted in the steel center of the earth! So it is with the Christian who, taking Holy Communion, is rooted even deeper in God's heart.

The scheduled Los Angeles-New York flight completes its circle over the ocean, points its chilly aluminum nose east, and is soon back over the mainland. Behind is Catalina Island in the ocean; below, the white surf on the Los Angeles beach; ahead, the mountains, snow-capped in winter, and beyond them lies the vast expanse of desert. I have made the flight often and have frequently noticed a tiny square patch of green in the middle of that seemingly endless desert wasteland—a thriving little farm surrounded by a thirsty monster of shifting sand. Will the defenseless little ranch be swallowed up by the parched desert? I doubt it. For this fertile oasis draws its life from deep wells that tap a subterranean river which finds its source in the high mountains. Far to the west, the snow on the mountains melts and the water streams silently down the eastern slope, draining deep into the sand to feed the subterranean river. The ranch is quite safe, for it has a secret alliance with the mountain!

So it is with the Christian who drinks deep from the wells of Holy Communion. His life is in the care and and keeping of God who stands in the shadows keeping watch above His own. Christian, you are an island surrounded by an unfriendly sea, a patch of green in a desert wasteland. But you will overcome. For in Christ, we are more than conquerors!

5

The Secret of Getting Divine Guidance

God penetrates our consciousness with sudden inspirations, unexpected brilliant moments and unexplainable illuminations! There are high moments in our lives when our minds are strangely alert, amazingly fertile, startingly productive, and ideas flow in a delightful and thrilling torrent of dynamic thought. We are shocked at our own extraordinary spiritual aliveness. How do you explain these times?

Still there are those who do not see the hand of God. How do you convince an illiterate person that the book placed in his hands contains a message! Or how can you prove to a person born deaf, dumb, and blind, that he is surrounded by sounds, colors, music and light?

"... he leadeth me in the paths of righteousness ... "

"H E GUIDES ME on the right track for his name's sake," is the way C.C. Briggs translates the classic line from the Twenty-Third Psalm. What remarkable confidence, what superior calmness, what extraordinary faith are expressed here! Whoever the poet is, he is very positive in his thinking, and steady in his soul: "He guides me on the right track."

Precisely, what is his faith? It is this—although he travels a long and perilous journey, he enjoys the presence of a Guide who keeps him from taking a dangerous turn off the right road. "Thy rod and thy staff they comfort me."

Unquestionably, decison-making is a major cause of anxiety. Few people can escape the responsibility of making decisions. And experience teaches us that what seems to be an insignificant decision oftentimes turns out to be a major resolution upon which our entire future turns and swings. Decisions are wild horses on which history often leaps to be carried sometimes for a long and wild ride. To illustrate: The year is 1919, the month is February. The place is France. The Big Four, Lloyd George, Clemenceau, Wilson and Orlando have been wrestling for months over the problem of the "peace" after World War I. What should they do with Russia? How must they handle Lenin who less than two years before had taken command of the Soviet Union? It is a crucial decision-making moment in history. One observer, Lewis Strauss, has recorded this incident. While the Big Four were wrestling with the question of Russia, a stormy young member of the British war cabinet made a fast trip across the choppy Channel to plead with the Big Four. He had an idea. Lewis Strauss writes, "He practically demanded an invasion of Russia by the Allies." But his advice was ignored. What did he know about such matters? He went back to England with his proposal rejected and ignored. His name was Winston Churchill. The decision was made. They would do nothing about Lenin or the Communists in Russia. And at that moment the history of the twentieth century took a flying leap upon a wild horse that has raced with crazy fury down through the treacherous years and today still carries the whole world along on a precarious ride. Tragic? Indeed! But does it not remind us of unfortunate decisions we have made in our own lives?

This brings us to the point at hand: Is it possible for a human being to be guided by supernatural wisdom in the decision-making moments of life? Christians, of course, claim that God is a living, invisible, personal Spirit who penetrates our mental consciousness and guides us. So we constantly pray for divine guidance when decisions must be made. We realize that the possibility of human error is almost infinite. Is this an opportunity that I am passing by? How shall I interpret these facts? How shall I judge this man? What tactics shall I take in this struggle? We often need the wisdom of Solomon! "He guides me on the right track." Ah, that is what we really need!

The hill country of Judea is wooded, rough terrain. The barren, sun-bleached hills are scarred by deep, ugly ravines as if some supercolossal beast had clawed deep gashes in the hillsides. In the canyon walls, black holes like the hollow eye sockets of a skull look down upon you. In these caves live wild animals and thieves. Traveling through these hills requires a guide. But the shepherd knows the hills and is able to guide his flock safely through dangerous territory. For he knows what lies on the other side of the hill. "He shall feed his flock like a shepherd . . . and gently lead those that are with young." So this Psalmist believed that as a shepherd is able to guide sheep safely through perilous and uncharted territory, so God is surely guiding His life on the right track.

But is it really true? The answer to that question depends largely upon our doctrine of man. For too long we have been deluged with a dialectical, materialistic doctrine of man which teaches that the human being is only an intelligent animal. We are taught that man is a biological, chemical organism with no soul, no spirit, and superior to animals only in the sense that we have a superior intelligence. Ideas that enter the brain can be explained naturally: they are stimulated by chemical activities within the body organism, triggered by past experiences, or stimulated by heredity or environment. In other words, all human thought processes can be analyzed and explained naturally.

Now, suddenly, from the University of Vienna in Austria comes a new psychology called logotherapy. Its founder, Dr. Victor Frankl, tells us that man has a spirit. As head of the Department of Psychiatry at this internationally famous university, he contends that there are a variety of uniquely human phenomena which human beings experience and which no other animal experiences. According to him man has a logos, or spirit. Man has the capacity for living in another dimension. Man has a conscience, which no other animal has. Intuition, instructive impulses, and imagination re-enforce his argument.

After spending several hours studying under this distinguished psychiatrist I arranged a private interview to ask him one question: "Dr. Frankl, I am delighted with your 'spiritual' concept of man. I have one question which I would like you to answer. *Why* is man made this way? What is the *cause* and the *reason* for this being? Why of all living organisms does the human being alone have the ability to feel conscience, to experience intuition, to receive intelligent impulses, to exercise imagination?" He placed both hands flat on his desk and gazed at me intently through his thin-rimmed glasses. He seemed perplexed, astonished, almost confused at the simple question, and finally answered, "I don't know. I don't know."

I walked out of his study confident. For I know the *why*. And so do you! To illustrate: I have many things in my office. There is a desk, a chair, a divan, a painting, a pen-and-pencil set, a typewriter, and a radio. Of all these things in my office only the radio is able to pick up messages and music out of the air. Why is the radio alone so gifted? The answer is incredibly simple—because the radio was *designed* to pick up messages from the air. Because there is music on the air waves and we want to pick it up we design an instrument to accomplish this purpose. And so God wanted one creature in His creation that would be able to pick up His divine messages and enjoy the music of the universe! So He created the human being with a mechanism designed to pick up spiritual signals. We call that mechanism the soul.

God penetrates our consciousness with sudden inspirations, unexpected brilliant moments and unexplainable illuminations. There are high moments in our lives when our minds are strangely alert, wide awake, amazingly fertile, startlingly productive, and ideas flow in a delightful and thrilling torrent of dynamic thought. We are shocked at our own extraordinary spiritual aliveness. How do you explain these times? When walking at night on an unfamiliar road, you are not sure of your path in the blackness until suddenly the clouds split to let a full moon illuminate the world around you clearly. You can see trees sleeping in the night, mountains standing strong around you, until the shifting clouds slide back across the golden moon and you are left in the dark again. But the light has shone long enough for you to get your bearings and you are able to move ahead with confident footing. So in an unexpected moment, God's Spirit illuminates our minds. A sudden inspiration we call it. And we have it—a big idea that may well prove to be a guideline for years to come. In the middle of the night we awaken and the answer to our problem, the right approach to our situation, the brilliant new idea is there clear and bright.

Sometimes God guides through what materialists would call coincidence. Check biographies to see how often this phrase appears, "The remarkable series of coincidences . . ." "By an extraordinary coincidence . . ." "A strange coincidence occurred . . ." "By an unexplainable coincidence . . ." By coincidence—which is to say, by no human intervention something happened which determined a destiny. Paths crossed. Strangers met for the first time. An encounter took place which was destined to change the entire course of a life, or a family, or a nation, or a world. Some people call it coincidence—the Christian calls it providence.

A few years ago I made plans for a world trip. At the same time another minister two thousand miles from my home made plans to take the same trip. Neither of us knew at the time that we would be traveling together. And by pure "coincidence" we were joined in a journey around the world. We lived together day after day and week after week. We rode camels together, crossed deserts together, grew weary and half-ill in Africa together. His name was Harold Leestma. Had it not been for that trip I am sure that he would not be in our church today as a minister of evangelism. Coincidence? No—God's guidance!

Sometimes God guides us through a sudden impulse or an

intuition. Helen Keller said to Philips Brooks that even though she was blind, deaf and dumb, she knew about God all the time. She just did not know his name. Is this divine guidance or intuition? Certainly positive, constructive, inspiring impulses that come out of the blue are often divine signals given to guide us. Suddenly we have an impulse to call a friend, to write a letter, or to turn into a street which we would normally never take, or cancel carefully made plans to take a trip, only to find that this seemingly unimportant decision changed the whole course of our lives! No doubt God is constantly transmitting signals through space to be picked up in our minds in the form of impulses. And the mind that is dialed to God and is on the celestial wave length will catch these signals and be guided thereby.

We all know that God guides us through our conscience, this "uniquely human phenomena" that we call the moral law within. "Let your conscience by your guide," we say. Again and again God pricks the human conscience to prod us down the right road.

God also guides through life's situations. Dr. Victor Frankl bases his entire psychology on the theory that "every situation in life has meaning." He says, "It is our responsibility to make a decision as to the meaning of these situations." Suddenly a door slams shut and a dream is crushed, hopes fade like dew in the noonday sun, and we are bitterly disappointed. But wait! There is a meaning for us in this situation. Perhaps God is using us in a most remarkable way to do some good that we are not aware of at all.

I have the honor of serving a pastor of the first walk-in-drive-in church ever to be built on the Pacific coast. We have a beautiful, million-dollar, award-winning church that is an inspiration to thousands of people. A thousand people can sit in a magnificent sanctuary. At the same time fifteen hundred people can worship in the privacy of their cars in a landscaped drive-in parking area of the church. Every Sunday parishioners crowd the sanctuary and cars to worship God. It is impossible to calculate the thousands of people who have heard a message of inspiration and hope from the gospel while in the privacy of their automobiles. The remarkable fact is that this church would never have been built had it not been for a totally paralyzed woman in her late seventies. We had originally begun our ministry in a drive-in theater with the intention of moving the entire congregation to a traditional sanctuary. Before our first sanctuary was erected, Rosie Gray was converted. She was totally paralyzed and could only worship in the drive-in church. There were indications that she would not live long. So the church board decided to conduct two services of worship, the first at nine-thirty on Sunday morning in the new sanctuary, and the second at eleven o'clock in the drive-in theater. "Until Rosie Gray died"—that was the plan. But she did not die. Months and years passed. Because of this situation a plan evolved—a plan to hire the world's best architect to build a combination "walk-in-drive-in" church where people could worship either in a sanctuary or in the privacy of their car. The idea caught fire. The policy was accepted. An architect was engaged. A down payment was made on ten acres of land. Plans were drawn. Money was collected. The contract to build the first walk-in-drive-in church on the Pacific coast was signed. Strange as it may seem, the day after ground-breaking—the day after the small congregation had made the public plunge to build a walk-in-drive-in church—Rosie Gray died! Finally the day of ground-breaking arrived. "They also serve who only stand and wait." One thing is certain: God used Rosie Gray to guide this young congregation to build a walk-in-drive-in church.

Still there are those who do not see the hand of God in human affairs! How can we make them see it? How do you convince an illiterate person that the book placed in his hands actually contains a message? Or how can you prove to a person born deaf, dumb, and blind, that he is surrounded by sounds, colors, music and light? Or how do you teach a man who has lived all his life in a cave that he actually has a shadow? He will not believe it unless he is able to get out of his darkness and stand in the sunshine. Which reminds us of Victor Hugo's classic remark, "Of course, there are those who do not believe in the Infinite: there are also those who do not believe in the sun, because they are blind."

To us who have felt the guidance of God in our life it is all very, very plain. So I say to you who struggle with skepticism, if you were to park your car in the parking lot of our church and saw before you a pile of lumber, a heap of rocks, sheets of glass, long strips of aluminum, and beams of steel, and suddenly, without a single human being intervening, you saw the wood float into the sky and join together, and at the precise moment beams of steel spontaneously soar into proper place, followed by flying strips of aluminum, then sheets of glass that slid through the sky like flying carpets, and everything finding its perfect place in a framework that was spontaneously erecting itself until before your very eyes you saw this modern sanctuary rise, take shape, and put itself together—what would you think? You would assume that there was some invisible intelligent force at work, planning everything and putting everything together!

It is thus that we view our universe, which is far more beautiful, far more complex, and far more orderly. No human being has ever laid claim to its design or its erection. There has been no human intervention whatsoever. Yet it is here, beautiful and organized.

Even more when we look upon our lives and we see a complexity of events, circumstances, situations, all fall into place through our years until we draw near to the end of life and we look back and say with certainty that there was a divine plan in all of these human events. Then we testify with the Psalmist, "He guided me in the right track."

How are we guided? The answer is no secret. Surely God

speaks to us through the Bible! Those who read it quietly and prayerfully find God's guidance. And prayer is still the mysterious experience where we tune our minds to the celestial wave length and ask God to guide us. In addition, there are thousands of people who will testify that in the quietness of worship God entered into their consciousness to illuminate them.

But I would suggest that the real secret of receiving Divine guidance is deeper than Bible reading, prayer, or worship. The key word is surrender. Surrender your sins, your self-centered desires, and your life to Jesus Christ. Surrender your mind to the Holy Spirit. Are you sure you want guidance? Would you take it if He gave it?

Do you know how to catch a dove? It is interesting that in the New Testament the dove is the symbol of the Holy Spirit. And the Holy Spirit is God who enters into our mental consciousness. Hundreds of thousands of visitors to the San Juan Capistrano Mission in Southern California try to catch the white doves that flock in the ancient mission. You may reach out with your hand, fingers open, and just as you are about to grasp the feet of the dove, it flaps its wings and flies away. So you try again. You reach out with your hand cautiously, slowly, furtively, and just as you are about to grab the bird, it escapes again. The secret is this: Simply extend your hand. Hold it out straight in front of you. Open your palm. Wait quietly. And the dove will come and rest right in the middle of your hand. Surrender your soul, your mind, your spirit that way to God. And He will take over your life and guide you. Something wonderful will happen. It may begin with a telephone call, a knock at the door, a "timely" article in this month's magazine, a sermon in church this coming Sunday, or the chance meeting of a new friend. "That's odd," you say. But I answer, "That's not odd—that's God!"

6

The Only Way to
Peace of Mind

Nothing can stop the man who feels the presence of God in his life. Terror is like morning dew in noonday sun. Fear is ice on summer seas. The tense, trembling, troubled heart becomes as placid and peaceful as water in an inland lake moments before the dawning of the day.

*"Yea, though I walk through the valley of
the shadow of death, I will fear no evil:
for thou art with me . . . "*

A WONDERFUL Christian woman recently described her experience with a group of nonreligious women in these words: "They all seemed to be trying to impress each other. I sensed stifling artificiality in the group. They all seemed to be so nervous."

That same day I was being interviewed by a reporter in my office at the Garden Grove Community Church. When I led the reporter into the huge glass cathedral, I noticed that she caught her breath in sudden surprise at the startling beauty of the church. She exclaimed spontaneously, "How tension-relieving!" Her comment brought to mind what Dr. Norman Vincent Peale whispered when he walked with me down the aisle of our church one Sunday morning, "I feel the presence of God here."

Take the three quotations from the three incidents and you have the theme of this chapter. "They all seemed so nervous."

"How tension-relieving!" "I feel the presence of God here." Real relief from tension and nervousness comes to the person who feels the presence of God. Peace of mind comes to the person who feels the presence of God.

No one has put it better than the Psalmist: "Yea, though I walk through the valley of the shadow of death, I will fear no evil: for thou art with me." This simple sentence has calmed more nervous souls, comforted more lonely people, encouraged more timid hearts than all the tranquilizers and psychiatrists put together!

Nothing can stop the man who feels the presence of God in his life. Terror is like morning dew in a noonday sun. Fear is ice on summer seas. The tense, trembling, troubled heart becomes as placid and peaceful as water in an inland lake moments before the dawning of the day. Abraham leaving his homeland to find a new country, Moses leaving Egypt to travel for forty years in the world's worst wilderness, Israel going to battle against pagan enemies—all found courage in the confidence that God was with them. The Israelites believed that God dwelled in the ark of the covenant. And when the ark was lost in a black moment of bitter battle, the news spread that the residence of God was stolen. Panic spread, hysteria replaced calm confidence, they lost their nerve and were defeated!

Imagine, if you will, what a humanly impossible situation the straggling followers of Jesus faced when He left them. They were a small band of unlettered men. Without a leader, they stayed together because of the promise of their Lord who had assured them, "Fear not, for lo, I am with you always, even unto the end of the world." For several days after the departure of Christ, this small band of disciples did nothing but wait in an upper room in Jerusalem, praying for an awareness of the presence and the power of God in their lives. Then something happened that changed the whole course of human history! God sent His Holy Spirit into their midst. It was an answer to a promise of Jesus who had assured them, "I will send you another Comforter." And moved with unbelievable courage, they faced an overwhelming enemy and turned the world upside down! They felt that God was not only with them— they felt that God was within them.

What did this do to their spirits? John said, "He that is in you is greater than he that is in this world." St. Paul felt that the presence of God in his life enabled him to do anything: "I am able to do anything through Christ who gives me great strength." I know of no truth more powerful once the human mind through faith has grasped its significance than the truth that God is actually with us if we so desire. Here is heaven in a sentence: "Thou art with me." And here is hell in a sentence: "My God, my God, why hast thou forsaken me?"

Are you suffering from great inner distress? Unimaginable peace can come into your mind by the time you reach the end of this chapter if you are aware that God is nearer than breathing and closer than hands or feet.

I have observed that people feel the presence of God in at least three different ways. For some people the presence of God is a mystical experience. Intuitively they sense that they are not alone. Have you ever had the feeling that someone was looking at you, or following you, and before you had a chance to turn around a friendly voice called out your name? How do you explain this? We call it intuition. Intuitively God makes His presence felt in the lives of many people. And we have a strong feeling that we are not alone in our car or in our house. We hear no voice. But silence has a voice all its own. It seems to speak of His presence.

Everytime I enter the pulpit of the Garden Grove Community Church to preach I pray that Christ will come to stand beside and behind me. I ask him to slip His arm around my shoulder. There have been times when His presence was awesome in its realism. I almost felt a pressure upon my shoulder. This has happened too often to be mere chance; in those moments words have spilled from my lips spontaneously to burn their way into the hearts of listeners who subsequently have been converted.

Mystically, we can experience the presence of God if we sharpen our spiritual capacity or sensitivity. It is like the mother who has a strange feeling that someone else is in the house and moments later her child calls out much to her surprise, for the hour is early and the child is normally not yet home from school. But before the mother heard the child's voice she had a sensation that she was not alone.

Take the case of a minister in our church who related this incident. He was called upon to visit a woman who never attended church but was looking for spiritual help because she was informed that she was in need of major surgery for what could well prove to be a malignancy. This was her story: "The day I received news of my need for major surgery I was tense and terribly troubled. That night I could not sleep. I went out for a ride in the car, and pulled into a gas station. The attendant who could not possibly have seen my face, for he came from the rear of the automobile, walked up to my door and before he saw me said to me, "Lady, are you in trouble?" He startled her. She stepped out of the car and they walked into the front office. The attendant said, "A voice inside of me said, 'You must talk to that woman. She's in trouble.'" He went on and added, "I don't go to church, but I think, lady, that it was God talking to me. I hope you don't think I'm crazy." She proceeded to tell him that she was in a deeply disturbed state of mind. And he continued to strengthen her spirit.

Sometimes we sense the presence of God in a mystical experience and sometimes in a deeply emotional experience. I recall an incident when Catherine Marshall-Le Sourd spoke to nearly four thousand people in our church in Garden Grove. In the closing minutes of her talk she said, "Join with me in this prayer," and she led the vast congregation in a prayer that God would come into the lives of people "tonight or tomorrow morning." The next morning at eleven o'clock one of the most intelligent women in the church, who had never had this kind of a deep religious experience, and was, in fact, always skeptical about emotional experiences, had a religious experience while at work in her kitchen! It was eleven o'clock on Monday morning, and this woman was overpowered by an awareness of the Holy Spirit. Though she was one who was never given to emotion, suddenly tears filled her eyes and bathed her face. She called me the next morning. I asked, "Well, how are you?", half-expecting her to challenge my previous Sunday morning sermon or argue a point of theology, which was her custom. But she said "Wonderful! Wonderful! Wonderful!" I said, "For goodness' sake, what's happened to you?" She answered, "At last I have found faith!" I spent three hours listening to her as she poured out her story. I am completely convinced that she had an authentic visitation from the Spirit of God!

Let us remember that there is nothing unscientific about deep emotion. God made the human being with the capacity for great emotional experiences in order that He might enter into the human life through this lifechanging channel. Wholesome emotional experiences are not to be scorned, or ridiculed, or belittled.

Sometimes God's presence is a mystical experience; sometimes it is a deeply emotional experience; more often it is subconscious confidence, a splendid assumption, a quiet sensation that you are not alone, a sanctified "taking it for granted that He is there" attitude, as you assume that the mountains are there hidden in the haze, lost in white shrouds of mist, but standing strong and majestic, though unseen.

From my home in Garden Grove, California, I can look out on a clear day and see the great Santa Ana Mountains. I remember a day when a friend from the East came to visit me. I had written to him about the beautiful mountains near our home. During the few days that he spent in our town mist and haze completely clouded the mountains. He never did see them. He

probably doubts that they are really there. The morning after
he left a rain cleared the atmosphere and suddenly there stood
the mountains again, so close, you could see the fire trails, and
tall trees towering into the sky, and the jagged outline of old
Saddleback rolling quietly under the sunrise! Suddenly their
presence was overpowering!

You may assume with a quiet subconscious confidence the
stars are still shining overhead at noonday even though you
do not see them. There is unquestioned confidence that they
have not left us. There is an unspoken assumption that, with
the passing of time and the coming of new darkness, they shall
make their appearance real once more. Or God's nearness is
like riding on a jet plane. You may never see the pilot, and
you may fly from New York to Los Angeles without hearing
his voice, but still, as you travel at supersonic speed, you are
completely relaxed, feeling the presence of the pilot in the great
plane even though you do not see him or hear him. You relax
in the tension-relieving assumption that someone is at the controls!

And if you tell me, "I don't believe in the presence of God,"
I would argue the point with you. You believe in the presence
of God more than you realize! Subconsciously your soul as-
sumes that as you speed through life on a whirling planet you
are not left to fate or fortune but deep down you take it for
granted that there is an Almighty God at the controls.

We would panic if we were told that there was no God at
the helm! Did you hear the story of the people who were on
a jet plane when over the intercom came this announcement,
"Good morning, gentlemen, you are part of a historic flight.
This is the first completely automated airplane. No human being is in control. Everything is under automation. We want
to assure you that there is absolutely nothing to worry, worry,
worry, worry . . . ."

Now for the crucial question—Why don't more people feel
this presence? In the first place, let us understand that God

cannot completely reveal His living presence to human beings. There is a verse in the Bible that I think must be interpreted absolutely literally: "No man shall see God and live." Of course! The physical organism would not be able to withstand the sheer excitement of a fully revealed experience with the living God. Our nervous system could not tolerate the thrill of it. One great Christian described the overpowering emotional experience of his conversion in these words, "Joy—joy—joy! Oh, the joy! I can hardly stand it!"

Somebody said to me once, "If there is a God, I wish He would show Himself." I answered, "If He did, you'd be dead!" As long as the soul is in the body, the human organism cannot survive the shock of total exposure to the full presence of God. The tremendous power of electricity that surges and flows through the electric wires must be drastically reduced through transformers before it is allowed in some small measure to enter into a little light bulb. The bulb just isn't big enough to take the full power.

But there are some people who do not seem to feel God's presence at all. Why? Perhaps the major reason is the fact that they do not want to feel God's presence. They don't experience it because they don't want to. St. John said, "They love darkness rather than light because their deeds are evil." The little boy who is up to mischief doesn't want his daddy to come around. And the housewife whose house is disorderly and unclean does not want company.

This explains why some people never go to church, or read their Bible, and, in fact, deliberately avoid Christian people, lest they expose their own lives to judgment! The way an overweight person avoids stepping on the bathroom scales, or the way an untidy person avoids looking in the mirror, or the way someone who has neglected his teeth avoids the dentist, or someone who hasn't paid his bills avoids the mail box—so some people are perfectly content not to have God come around!

Do you know how God punishes us for this? By giving us

exactly what we want: He leaves us alone! And that's the beginning of hell on earth!

But how about good people who have trouble feeling God's presence? For many, I suspect, the world gets in the way. Brains become barriers. Eyes and ears become obstacles. The blind ploughman wrote, "God took away my eyes that my soul might see!" There is good reason why men close their eyes when they pray! "The world knoweth him not, for it seeth him not; but ye know him, for he dwells in you," was Christ's word on this point.

And how do you explain religious people who have trouble feeling God's presence? What is their problem? Who knows? Perhaps God deliberately limits His revelation in order to keep us from becoming "so heavenly minded that we are no earthly good." I have observed, however, that there are three reasons why religious people lack the awareness of God's presence. One reason is that some people keep trying to ride along through life on an old religious experience. This just does not work. The great Christian experience you had cannot last long before it will have lost its luster.

The sanctuary of the Garden Grove Community Church is a hundred and forty feet long. The walls are entirely made of glass. Slowly, suddenly, the clearness of the glass becomes clouded through a collected film that adheres to the glass bit by bit until the sunshine no longer shines through sparkling and golden. The windows need to be washed. The film needs to be cleansed away. Life has a way of putting a film over our old religious experiences until we can no longer see God clearly. We need a new experience with Him! One small group of Christian people that meets regularly always makes the announcement before every meeting, "What new experience have you had with God this past week? We don't want to hear your old stories!"

How can we have fresh experiences with God? The answer to this question will suggest a second reason why some religious people do not experience God's presence. St. James brings the point forcibly home, "Faith without works is dead." One reason why many religious people do not feel the presence of God is that they are not doing anything for him. When did you really go out of your way to do something wonderful, thoughtful, generous, and really kind for someone?

A third reason why many religious people do not feel the presence of God is that they still have their self on the throne. They believe in God. They pray to God. They worship God regularly. But they have never, never abdicated themselves! They are so wrapped up in their own self that they do not feel the presence of God. One day recently I came home with a pile of work from my office. I had received that day from the architect's office photographs of a scale model of the Tower of Hope which we are planning to build on our church property. I sat in my overstuffed chair in the family room of my home and looked over the assorted pictures that had come from the architect and thrilled to this magnificent seventeen-story tower to be built from glass and gleaming aluminum. I was dreaming about the little chapel in the sky which would occupy the seventeenth floor of this beautiful tower. I was dreaming about the twenty-four-hour prayer room in this top floor, where members of our church would be in twenty-four-hour, three-hundred-sixty-five-day prayer session to receive emergency calls from people with problems. I was dreaming about the staff of Christian psychological counselors that would fill several offices in the Tower of Hope to counsel and comfort hundreds of thousands of people in years to come. And I was dreaming about ways in which to raise a million dollars to build this fabulous tower of Christian hope. I was not aware of the fact that I was sitting in my chair. Suddenly I heard a loud voice in my ear and I said, "Don't shout at me! What is it, Bobby?" There was Bobby, my nine-year-old son. He had been talking to me, but I had never heard him. He had been standing there for a long time and I had never seen him. Why? I was totally unaware of his presence because I was so wrapped up in my own project! Ah! That's the nub of it! God is standing right at our side, and speaking to us all the time, but we are so wrapped up in our own projects and plans that we never feel His presence or hear His voice!

I think you can see now what you have to do to have a vital experience with God, who is close to you even as you read these words. Stop thinking about yourself, stop worrying about yourself, stop imagining the world revolves around you! But be careful! You may be converted! You may even have a great emotional experience! But a man must be "born again before he can enter into the kingdom of God." Listen to the testimony of the Rev. Edward L. R. Elson. He relates his personal experience in the book *The Inevitable Encounter.* He tells how he met Jesus Christ. "At midnight we were on our knees in prayer. Somehow that night Jesus Christ came, searched me out, lighted up the hidden corners of my soul, exposed the emptiness and littleness of my youthful heart and let His light in so that I knew what I ought to be through Him. And when I asked Him to forgive me, He did. When I asked Him to fill my soul with life and power, He did. Something deep and unutterable overflooded me that night. I knew that I would never, never be alone again. I wanted to love everybody. I promised Him I would go where He wanted me to go, be what He wanted me to be. Nothing seemed too great or too impossible for this Friend."

You may have a similar experience when you turn your life over to Jesus Christ. You will know down deep in your heart that you will never, never, never, be alone again.

Still there may be times when you do not feel God's presence. For a moment you may be almost terrified at His apparent absence. But when your life is at its worst, God will meet you in the blackest moments, and you will grow strangely quiet and peaceful, knowing that you are not walking alone.

That great Scottish preacher, John McNeill, related how as

a young lad he worked late on Saturdays. To reach home he would have to walk through seven dark, dangerous miles on a road that was infamous for robbers and thieves. "One Saturday it was past midnight before I finished my work and left for home. Two miles out of town the road got blacker than ever. There were high, wooded hills on the right and high, wooded hills on the left. The night was as black as a wolf's jaw. I was sixteen years old. I was moving along so fast that my feet hardly touched the ground. Then, suddenly, twenty yards in front of me, so it seemed, there rang out a great, strong, manly voice. 'Is that you, Johnny?' And for a moment I couldn't really have told you my name! And then I recovered. That was my father come to meet me at the worst of it! His voice first startled me and then delivered me from all my fears. The night became light around me! His hand on my shoulder, his voice in my ear, and his feet rising, falling on the road beside my own, I feared no evil, for he was with me. I can't tell you anymore about the road home that night. Why? Because I was as good as home right there. All that makes home home was with me!" "Yea, though I walk through the valley of the shadow of death, I will fear no evil; for thou art with me."

7

Your Future Is Your Friend

The hand of the Almighty is never far away. No wonder you can trust the future! And when you cannot see any good, but only stark, naked, cruel, brutal tragedy in a catastrophic situation, then you can expect God to come and show mercy! As an unexpected gust of wind comes under the weary wings of a storm-drenched bird to lift the pitiful creature to higher altitudes where it can soar in new strength, so God comes with an unannounced invasion of mercy.

*"Surely goodness and mercy shall
follow me all the days of my life . . . "*

MATILDA WAS a cheerful maid who worked for a wealthy woman who was a chronic worrier. One day the mistress questioned her overly plump and disgustingly cheerful maid, "Matilda, do you have any money in the bank?" "No, ma'am, but I get along on what I get." "But, Matilda, suppose you get sick? Or suppose we should lose our investments and would have to let you go, and suppose you wouldn't be able to find another job?" At that point the wonderful Christian maid interrupted with a blunt sermon in her own style, "Suppose, suppose, suppose. That's all you ever do! There's no supposing in my Bible! My Bible says, 'Surely goodness and mercy shall follow me all the days in my life, and I shall dwell in the house of the Lord for ever.'" And then, in a final burst of beautiful exhortation, the maid declared, "That's your trouble, Mrs., you is doing too much supposing and not enough reposing!"

77

What security is expressed in this sentence: "Surely goodness and mercy shall follow me all the days of my life"!

What's that, you say? This Psalmist did not have to worry about cancer, or Communism, or thermonuclear war, or airplane crashes, or highway accidents, or labor-management conflicts? Wait a minute! Maybe not. But let us not forget that this was the day of pestilence, plagues, famines, leprosy, blindness, slavery, swords, spears and arrows! And perhaps a greater threat—this was the day when men were expected to have two, three and sometimes four wives!

It is hard to believe that the man who writes with such inner security lived before the time of water-purification plants, public disposal systems, fire engines, and hospitals! He lived in a day when the average life span was in the twenties, when many women died nine months after they were married, and the odds favored the death of their new-born child. This was the day when epileptics were dammed as devil-possessed people, eccentric women were burned as witches, and lawbreakers' eyes were gouged out and their tongues cut off for petty crimes. The Psalmist demonstrates a faith that would make many a modern American's faith look pretty sick by comparison. It is obvious that he had a profound faith in God.

Why don't we have it? We have touched upon reasons in the earlier chapters. Permit me to add an additional reason at this point. It is not that we find ourselves unable to believe in God. The problem seems to be our inability to comprehend and truly believe that God is able to keep a watchful eye on each living individual. It is easy to believe that God is concerned about important people who hold high positions and power in world affairs. But is God genuinely concerned and interested in me? A.J. Cronin frankly confessed that this was his obstacle to faith while he was in medical school. But in his study of the brain and nervous system a beautiful faith came into his life. Here is the reasoning which helped him: Within the human body there are millions of nerve endings. And there is one great brain. The mind is occupied with big thoughts, until the finger is pricked with a pin or the thorn of a rose. Then suddenly the mind which is capable of far more lofty, sweeping, and important thoughts is preoccupied with the thorn in the tip of a little finger! Is it not possible that by some mysterious, unexplored, undetected cosmic arrangement God is able to maintain a lively connection with every living human being, and that when you and I are hurt, God feels it, and knows it?

Is God the master mind of the universe, and are you and I the millions of nerve endings? In an overcollectivized type of society, are we not in danger of underestimating the significance of the individual? Have we forgotten that no two people are exactly the same? When a machine manufactures its product it turns out identical products by the millions. Not so with God! No two human beings have ever been created exactly alike. Why not? Is God trying to demonstrate His personal concern over each distinctive individual person? The whole science of finger printing proves that no two people are identical. If the FBI in Washington, D.C., is able to determine in a matter of minutes the identity and the character of an individual by a finger print, is it inconceivable that God lacks a spiritual arrangement whereby He is able to know each distinctive person whom He has allowed to be born?

Now take a good look at this man's faith. What does he believe, and what is he saying? He is not saying that he expects no trouble or problems. He frankly anticipates walking through the valley of the shadow of death. There is no promise that because God knows each individual that we will all live placidly past eighty, and die peacefully in our sleep. There is no assurance that we shall never fly through a windshield on the freeway, or be lucky enough to miss the airplane that happens to fall in the East River, or that our children will never be struck by a car, or brought low by leukemia, or have to go to war and maybe die there.

Then what does the Psalmist mean by saying that goodness and mercy will follow him all the days of his life? He is saying that he has no anxiety or fear of the future. He is convinced that in the providence of God the future will be friendly.

Fear poverty? No—"The Lord is my shepherd, I shall not want." Fear loneliness? No—"For thou art with me." Fear a nervous breakdown? No—"He will make me lie down in green pastures beside still waters." Fear falling into terrible sin? No—"Thy rod and thy staff they comfort me." Fear making bad judgments? No—"He leadeth me." Fear life, death, and eternity? No—"I shall dwell in the house of the Lord for ever."

"Surely goodness and mercy shall follow me all the days of my life." Sweet words! Like the note of a nightingale, or gentle music that falls from a harp! Strong words! Like a chorus of men's voices singing on Easter morning. Triumphant words! Like a great pipe organ swelling to full power in the mighty closing moments of a thrilling magnificat!

The Psalmist claims that he is not afraid of the future because he believes that God is good. For many of us this is easy to believe. We count our blessings—blessings of country, family, friends, eyes, hands, and ears. The goodness of God is very conspicuous to His unspoiled children.

But, admittedly, there are times when it is hard to believe in the goodness of God. Sometimes there are clouds that hide the smiling face of God. Love wears many faces. Sometimes the goodness of God is hidden behind His frowning face. What appears to be a tragedy turns out to be a blessing in disguise. The November 1963, issue of the *Reader's Digest* tells the story of a man who learned to paint beautiful pictures after he was totally blind. Impossible? Seemingly, but it is true!

I think of a member of a former church that I served. This gentleman developed cancer of the larynx. A laryngectomy had to be performed. He was left without a voice box. But he managed to learn to speak with a special electronic gadget.

And he capitalized on his calamity. He turned this liability into an asset. He was able to gain a great deal of attention through this novel invention. At the same time he cultivated his sense of humor. I remember one night when a large group of people were meeting in a home. The laughter and talk was loud. We suddenly heard what sounded like a siren. It was Bill Bruin, the voiceless man, making an imitation of a siren on his electronic voice box. He was having lots of fun with his liability!

About that time I began to wonder and worry what I would do if I should ever have to undergo a laryngectomy. As a pastor of a church my voice is an indispensable tool. Then I reflected on the mysteries of God's goodness and relaxed in the peace-generating idea that if God ever permitted me to undergo an laryngectomy, it would undoubtedly be His way of getting me out of one position into a more fruitful job!

Sometimes the goodness of God is stern. "Thy rod and thy staff they comfort me." Discipline is goodness, too! A father has often been his best when he made his child cry! The little girl is crying because her daddy will not let her ride the bike on the street after dark! Or a son is deeply hurt because his father will not let him take the car on a crowded holiday highway. When the shepherd uses his rod and staff to strike the sheep before it runs down a dangerous trail or off a precipice, is not the shepherd good indeed?

And often God is good in ways beyond our knowledge. God does so much for us that we never know about! His goodness *"follows"* me. That means that we never see a great deal of good that God does as He follows in our track. It is like a mother or a father who picks up after the children long after they are asleep in their beds. A son plants his little flower in the garden and does a poor job of it. After he has gone to the street to play, his father finishes the job, and corrects his son's mistakes. But the son never knows it, and the flower grows and blooms. Weeks later the son calls his friends in and brags

81

about his expert gardening. He does not realize that the plant would have withered and died if his father had not replanted it in soft, moist soil.

God is always picking up after us. Recently a lady came into my office with regrets. She was miserable worrying about mistakes she had made in her lifetime. "Did you ever ask God to forgive you?" I asked. "Oh, yes," she answered. "Then forget about it," I told her, continuing, "I will not even pray about it this morning. I will not even ask God to forgive you your mistakes. If you could go back and find the people you have offended you would discover that they have forgotten all about it. They would say that time has healed the wounds. The truth is that God has been following after you and has corrected your mistakes."

Still there are some apparent human tragedies that defy the imagination; we cannot see the goodness of God in these catastrophes. The week that I wrote this chapter there was an explosion in an ice rink in Indianapolis, Indiana, that claimed sixty-four lives. Can you tell the survivors at a time like this that God is good? What can we say when there is no evidence of God's goodness? What can we say when with all our positive thinking we cannot possibly see anything good in what has happened? *Then God will show His other face. And this is the face of mercy.* Nothing will ever happen to you unless it is good, good for you, good for God, good for someone else. If anything ever befalls you that does not appear to be good for you, for God, or for anyone else, but is only the result of sin of some terrible blunder, then you can expect a redeeming sympathy and the kiss of God's tender mercy. And if God will come to comfort, you and I can take anything!

In the course of a day's herding of sheep there are some sheep that will be cut, scratched, and wounded. At night the shepherd gives these sheep his special attention. He reaches for his horn of olive oil and cedar tar and tenderly bestows his healing mercy. "Thou anountest my head with oil." As a mother who rises at night to carry and comfort her feverish baby, so God comes to the tragedy-shocked soul to bestow mercy. At the darkest time in life, and at the weariest moment of our existence, when it appears that God has forsaken or forgotten us, when we cannot comprehend or see evidence of the goodness of God, he will come and bestow mercy and tenderness. If, in your time of tragedy, you will cling with a childlike faith to God He will visit you with a tender kiss of mercy.

I remember a day when I endured a weird assortment of irritations, conflicts and tensions. I finally arrived home at five-thirty, went to my bedroom, tried in vain to relax, and prayed without any apparent relief. Then suddenly God answered my prayer in a most remarkable way. My bedroom door opened. Slowly, cautiously, my little girl peeked through the opening of the doorway. Her big brown eyes appeared through the slot in the door and, judging that it was safe, she suddenly threw the door wide open, ran to the edge of the bed, and the next thing I knew her soft silky hair was flowing over my eyelids and caressing my lips. Her soft cheek was on mine. She kissed and hugged me, then drew swiftly back as if she was expecting me to say, "What do you want?" And she said, "I just wanted to kiss you, because I love you, Daddy." And abruptly she whirled out, skipping and running, and the door closed behind her. She was gone, but I found myself relaxed. I drew strength from this unexpected invasion of affection. So God comes at the trying time with an unexpected shower of tenderness.

What then is my faith? I believe with this Psalmist that there is an unseen God at the controls of the life that has been surrendered to Him. God will let nothing happen unless it is for our own good or for the good of God's Kingdom, or for the good of others.

Make no mistake about it, there is another hand above your own! My son was nine years old and wanted badly to learn to drive my car. I let him sit between my legs and permitted

83

his hands to grip the wheel and steer the car around the ten-acre church grounds. His little white-knuckled hands strangled the steering wheel but he managed to manuever the turns, and bring the powerful automobile back to the parking space. When we came home to lunch, you should have heard him boast to his mother and older sister! "I drove the car, Mommy, all by myself! Really, I did!" Happy, but foolish child! I had my big hands only a fraction of an inch over his all the time, ready to clamp down and take over in case I sensed him losing control. And, unknown to him, all the while *my* foot was on the gas pedal.

No, friend, you are not left alone at the controls of your life! I recall an incident when my little girl insisted on pouring her own milk from a heavy pitcher. "Let me pour it, please!" she begged. Finally we let her chubby fingers take hold of the narrow top of the brimful pitcher and she actually thought that she lifted the weight, and poured the milk without spilling it, all by herself! She never noticed that I had slipped my hand under the moist bottom of the heavy pitcher and lifted the weight, nor did she notice that my hand remained there to steer the point of the pitcher to the glass and to restrain the lowering of the heavy load when she prepared to put it down.

The hand of the Almighty is never far away. No wonder you can trust the future! And when I cannot see any good, but only stark, naked, cruel, brutal tragedy in a catastrophic situation, then I can expect God to come and show mercy! As an unexpected gust of wind comes under the weary wings of a storm-drenched bird to lift the pitiful creature to higher altitudes where it can soar in new strength, so God comes with an unannounced invasion of mercy!

Mercy is the declaration that our sins are forgiven. Mercy is the sudden glimmer of something new to live for. Mercy is the slender sliver of silver hope through the dark night. Mercy is the first faint, then growing, thought that I must, I will, pick up the pieces and start over again!

Your Future is Your Friend

You want to argue the point? I refuse! It's a choice—not an argument. It must be a decision—not a debate! G. Studdert Kennedy said: "These clouds are lies. They cannot last. The blue sky is the truth, for God is love. Such is my faith, and such my reasons for it, and I find them strong enough. And you? You want to argue? Well, I can't. It is a choice and I choose the Christ."

You can go through life a cynic and a doubter if you choose. Many people do. Remember Miss Havisham in *Great Expectations*? She was to be married. The guests arrived. The wedding cake adorned the elaborate table. She was lovely in white lace. But the bridegroom never came. Finally, in deep desperation she sent the guests home. It was twenty to nine. She made a choice. She would not accept her loss. All clocks were stopped at twenty to nine. All drapes were drawn and sunlight was shut out. The cake was left on the table. She decided that there would be no future for her. She stopped the clocks! The picture that is painted in the succeeding chapters is pitiful. The wedding cake hardens under gathering cobwebs and thick dust. A flickering candle is the only light in the gloomy room. The flame seems to laugh and mock her folly! Her wedding gown grows yellow over her shrunken figure. She grows old, bitter and miserable!

You can choose to believe that way if you want. Not I! I like the attitude of my neighbor. She and her husband worked, saved, and in their fifties bought a lovely home two doors east of our house. How hard they worked to move the furniture in Rent-All trailers. Boxes, suitcases, crates of furniture crowd her home and her back yard as I write this chapter. Suddenly, one week after they moved, her husband, without warning, died from a heart attack! And she was left alone with the large new home. I stopped to talk to her one morning. She was out in the yard surveying the boxes, barrels, and unpotted plants. The morning was bright. She looked wide awake as she took stock of the work that needed to be done. I said, sympathetically, "How are you today, Mrs. Ford?" She smiled, "Quite well, thank you, Reverend. You know what gives me great strength? It is the certain assurance that it was my husband's time to go. It was God's will. And it is His will for me to get these plants in the ground and things unpacked!" A false front? Or did she mean it? The next day she was helping the neighborhood children collect old newspapers for the paper drive in the local school! She was laughing and pulling the wagon overflowing with newspapers. And only two days ago she was in our home for coffee with the ladies of the neighborhood. She said, "Oh, sometimes I cry—but it was God's will. And I know He loves me. He does nothing wrong."

Her life has not stopped. She goes on building, planning and spreading cheer. As I watch her, I remember these words, "I had fainted unless I had believed to see the goodness of the Lord in the land of the living."

Here's a gallant faith for you. Choose it! There is no self-pity, no jealousy, no cynicism, no pessimism, no complaining, no criticizing, no gloominess here. "Surely goodness and mercy shall follow me all the days of my life." Use a trumpet or a harp when you sing these words. Let the world keep its saxophones—and its blues!

Two things the future holds for me—and for you, Christians: (1) Goodness; in sunshine and shadow, goodness all the way; (2) Mercy; when I cannot see or comprehend or perceive any goodness, then I will experience the kiss of God's comforting presence. Years later we may see it and say, "It is good for me to have been in trouble" (Ps. 119:71, Moffatt).

You want to believe it, but can't? You want more reasons? Why does this trouble have to happen to you, you ask? *But that is one question God seldom answers.* Christ asked it on the cross and God never answered His question, "My God, my God, *why* . . . ?" Remember, the road of reason ends with a question mark. And the road of faith ends with an exclamation mark!

You know the Twenty-Third Psalm; but do you know the Shepherd? You know the Psalm; but do you know the first two words? Do you know "the Lord"?

Draw close to Jesus Christ, and once you fill your mind with His words and your life with His spirit, you will have a new burst of faith and you will never doubt that your future is your friend!

8

Some People
Never Die

The truth is that Jesus Christ gave His life to tell us the truth about life after death. And what is His report? Let us listen to Him. I suggest that you are on far safer ground believing Him than believing your doubts. His first statement and His first report is that the human being has an immortal soul which survives the physical experience called death. He said, "He that lives and believes on me shall never die."

*" . . . And I will dwell in the house
of the Lord for ever . . . "*

WHAT A TOWERING FOUNTAIN is to a park, and a rose
window is to a cathedral, and the key diamond is to
the point of a crown, that is what this sentence is to this royal
Psalm. It is a soul-thrilling, heart-lifting, eye-moistening, faith-
generating sentence: "And I will dwell in the house of the Lord
for ever." Which brings to my mind an impertinent, impetu-
ous, proud professor who said not long ago in my hearing,
"It is now scientifically proved that there is no heaven and there
is no hell." The poor fool! I forgot about him until quite recently. I was driving along one of our two-lane blacktop roads
that is called upon to carry four-lane traffic. As I rode along
this narrow, dangerous street, I saw on the side of the road
a stiff-kneed, snowy-haired, trembling old man. In one hand
he hugged a paper sack out of which peeked the top of a loaf
of bread. He embraced it tightly as if it steadied and supported
him somehow. In the other hand he was holding the banner

of blindness, a white rubber-tipped cane, with which he fingered cautiously the crumbling edge of the uncurbed blacktop road which told him whether he was still on the side or whether he was wandering into the oncoming traffic. I looked at him as I drove slowly by; I could almost see the weary eyelids twitching and trembling over his unseeing eyes. The sight of him made me nervous, for there were cars coming too fast toward him and I hoped he would not miss his white-caned cue and wander into the oncoming traffic. I wanted desperately to stop and offer him a lift. But I thought my offer might offend his dignity. So I drove on. And then, strangely enough, I was suddenly reminded of that proud, impertinent professor who denied belief in life after death. He, too, was stumbling dangerously and blindly out of his own field of safe knowledge into the realm of religion. And he was teaching as facts what were only his negative assumptions. It reminded me of the very ordinary joke about an old farmer who confronted an arrogant agnostic with this comment: "Just 'cause you say there ain't no hell ain't no sign you ain't going there."

There are a variety of doctrines, opinions, and philosophies about life after death. But they all fall into three major categories, and you may take your choice. Let us look at them briefly.

You can be a nihilist, believe in nothing, as does that impertinent professor. According to this theory, when you die, you are dead, a candle blown out. It would be more accurate to say that man is more like a moon that reflects and mirrors the sun. William James said that many of the thoughts in the human experience and the human existence are not thoughts produced by the gray matter under the skull, but they come from outer space and the spiritual universe in which we live. The mind does not produce all of its thoughts—it just transmits some of these thoughts, not like a sun that generates its own light, but like a moon that is reflecting other light that comes from without. And James goes on to say, "It is impossible for me or for any psychologist to determine whether the ideals and the obsessions and the compulsions in the mind of a man are produced in his own brain or whether they are impulses and ideas that are being transmitted through him from outside." But you can believe as the nihilists believe. A nihilist believes there is nothing. Everything is annihilated, done away with, obliterated. That would be heaven for people who live a devil of a life! In fact, it would be a rather universal injustice to think that some people could get so neatly off the hook!

Well, there is another idea. It is that the soul survives death and enjoys elation; there is a heaven and everybody goes there, because God is so loving and so kind that He would not let anyone miss it. Presumably even Adolf Hitler and the butchers who burned the millions of Jews go there because God is all-loving. Frankly, if that were the case, I think I'd want to be counted out!

Then there's a third view, and for this belief let us go to the person that I consider to be the authority on the subject, and that is Jesus Christ. Now, let us assume that Colonel John Glenn gave a lecture to tell what it was like in outer space and that he described the sights and pictured for us very dramatically what the world looked like from up there. After his detailed lecture let us presume that I stepped forward and said, "Now, just a minute, Mr. Glenn, I want to challenge what you say." Who would believe me instead of Colonel John Glenn who has been there and has come back to tell us about it? The truth is that Jesus Christ gave His life to tell us the truth about life after death. And what is His report? Let us listen to Him. I suggest that you are on far safer ground believing Him than believing your doubts. His first statement and His first report is that the human being has an immortal soul which survives the physical experience called death. He said, "He that lives and believes on me shall never die." Now, there you have it.

I suppose some people have difficulty believing this in our

agnostic world, because they think of the human being as merely another animal. And it is true. We have animalistic bodies in the sense that we eat like animals; we see and we smell and we taste and we reproduce—in that sense, we are animals. I remember a biologist who said to me, "I would like to show you the embryo of a monkey and the embryo of a human being." He was one of those agnostics. He said, "You can't tell the difference!" He's right. You can't. If you saw the embryo of a monkey and the embryo of a human being, you could not tell the difference. They are that much alike. My answer to him was simple. The difference is in what they are becoming! One will grow up to be nothing but a hairy monster! The other will grow up to have the gift of intelligence, intuition, creativity and what Victor Frankl, the psychiatrist, calls noesis, or a noetic quality, and what the Bible calls the soul and the spirit. That's the difference!

This reminds me of a very interesting story. You may have heard it. There was a Western farmer who on a mountain hike found an egg lying in the grass. He picked it up, took it home, and put it under the hen that was sitting on chicken eggs. Eventually the hen hatched the egg along with the other eggs. But what come forth was the most awkward, crude, ugly-looking creature the farmer ever saw. He called the neighbors in and asked if they knew what it was but they could not tell. Nobody had the slightest idea what this peculiar creature was. It developed wings that became a heavy burden on the little body—big oversized, clumsy wings that were too big for him. And its legs developed deformed crooks that looked like claws, and the beak, instead of being straight and sharp was crooked. It survived and it grew until one day, above the barnyard, there was a shrill scream and this awkward bird looked up and he saw gliding slowly in great circles above the farmyard a huge bird; and for the first time, his instinct told him what he was. He was an eagle—bred for the mountains, born to fly, and destined never to be happy while earth-bound in a barnyard.

Ah, that's it. Why do human beings have such frustrations, such disturbances, such mental problems? We may have legs and we may have mouths and we may have eyes like animals. But we are bred for heaven. And so, St. Augustine said, "No human being is really at peace until he has come to God by faith." We instinctively feel the call of eternity, like the wild, domesticated animal who hears the call of the wild and must respond. One wise philosopher said that when God wants to prove something to people He puts it in their instincts. So that is Christ's first word on the subject; we are born for eternity.

Then he goes on and He says something quite specific. He says there is a hell out there. At this point we ought to remember that the whole idea of hell was taught by the gentlest, tenderest, sweetest Person who ever lived. And the talk about outer darkness and the closed door and the weeping and the gnashing of teeth and the lake of fire and other figurative expressions also fell from the lips of the most compassionate Person who ever lived.

But that kind of talk is outdated now, isn't it? Wait a minute, maybe it isn't outdated. Leslie Weatherhead, who is considered a liberal British theologian, had these words to say: "Sin is a terrible thing in the universe. Let us never forget that though the idea of hell has been caricatured in a fantastic vulgarity by the generation of our great-grandfathers, we are doing our generation a greater disservice if we make light of sin and pretend that it does not matter and that you are all going to the same place and that God will pat everybody on the head and say finally, 'There, there, it doesn't matter. I am sure you didn't mean it. Come, now, and enjoy yourselves.' We need," Mr. Weatherhead said, "to remember that the most terrible things ever said were spoken by the most wonderful person who ever lived." And Peter Marshall, in a book that Catherine, his wife, published, puts it this way: "We must never forget that the lust to pain, the tendency to abuse sex, the crave to drink are evil desires; first, not of the body but of the frustrated spirit. And the spirit survives death. Suppose," Marshall continues, "these grand souls still have their desires and lusts, their passions and their cravings still gnawing, eating and burning constantly at their personalities. Suppose in eternity they still have their desires and no bodies to gratify these desires. Would that not be hell?" Or imagine that someday your soul and mine stand completely naked before God, completely stripped of all of the things that made us feel secure and confident in this life. Would that not be hell?

An allegory tells about a soul that came to heaven. Just outside of heaven was a huge arena called "The Court of Status Symbols." Before he could get into heaven he had to go through this area, past the keeper of the door of the court. Inside he saw sleek automobiles, membership cards to exclusive clubs, white poodles, silver-tipped canes, etc. As he went farther back into the room he saw the crowns of kings and beautiful jewelry from princesses. Then the guide said, "Yes, these were all things that the world used to impress people, symbols of significance. But they don't impress Him! So we have everybody drop them right here before they come to stand before Him!"

For some people, I submit, to have to stand before God without all of the props that we have been using to impress people might be a nightmare. Or suppose, as a certain theologian suggested, that death is like a dream. Imagine that death will be like falling asleep. Suddenly you awake to an unending dream! We know, of course, that dreams for the most part are exaggerated projections of our past experiences. For one who has lived in the love of God and has thrilled to beautiful music and has felt the wonderful warmth of faith, life after death will be one long, beautiful, unending and inspiring dream. But for one to whom existence has been nothing more than self-indulgence, feeding the desires of his physical organism which can no longer be fed in eternity, would not the dream be one unending nightmare? So Christ makes the point clear. There is hell; there is heaven.

Now against this sober background, one important question

looms large. Are you saved? Your eternity is determined by you in your lifetime. How? By the life you live? To some extent, I suppose, but that is not really all. None of us can really atone for the sins we have committed. Then how can we be redeemed or saved? I know of only one Person in all of human history who ever said, "I am the good shepherd. By me, if any man enter in, he shall be saved." His name is Jesus Christ.

Indeed, there have been many religious leaders. There have been many philosophers in the stream of human history, but no one ever dared to say, as Christ said, "I am the way, the truth and the life. No man cometh unto the Father but by me."

So, this is how! You simply come to Christ. It means that you must admit that you have sinned and need salvation. "A broken and a contrite heart, O God, thou wilt not despise."

Understand this. God has never sent a single soul to hell. He never has and He never will! Men send themselves there by proudly refusing to accept His gift of love. Christ will save anybody who comes. "Him that cometh unto me," He said, "I shall under no circumstances cast out."

Someday I shall have to cross the dividing line and move to the other side, and so will you. Personally, I anticipate it as the most exciting trip I have ever taken and I anticipate it with more excitement than I did my first around-the-world trip a number of years ago. "I have no fear, for thou art with me."

"Him that cometh unto me I will in no wise cast out." And what does it mean to come? It doesn't mean just to sit and politely ignore Him. It means to rise up and accept Him. "Someday," John McNeil said, "I will draw my feet into the bed for the last time and turn my face to the wall and I will have to look at the gulf, but my Shepherd and I will look at it together. 'I will fear no evil, for him that cometh unto me I will in no wise cast out.' I will hold onto that and dare to swing out over the wide gulf on that slender rope, knowing that it will not drop me, for it is rooted in God's imperishable love." Take hold of that rope now!